TEXTILE
Artistry

TEXTILE
Artistry

Edited by
VALERIE CAMPBELL-HARDING

Chilton Book Company
Radnor, Pennsylvania

Originally published in Great Britain in 1994
by B. T. Batsford Ltd, 4 Fitzhardinge Street, London W1H 0AH
under the title *Starting to Stitch Creatively*

British Library Cataloguing-in-Publication Data.
A catalogue record for this book is available
from the British Library

ISBN 0-8019-8780-6

Printed in Hong Kong

Jacket illustration:
Details of the projects in this book

Page 3
A detail of the ribbon and fabric pansy bags on page 34

CONTENTS

THE AUTHORS

Valerie Campbell-Harding trained at Chippenham Technical College, and then at Goldsmith's College in London and Loughborough Art College. She is the Editor of *The World of Embroidery*, and of the magazine of the Computer Textile Design Group, which she founded. She teaches City & Guilds Embroidery at two colleges, lectures, exhibits and holds embroidery workshops all over the UK. She is the author of eight books on embroidery and design, and is co-author of two more with Pam Watts (published by B.T. Batsford).

Gail Harker is a Canadian now living in England. She holds City & Guilds Parts I and II and L.C.G.I., and is a Verifier for City& Guilds. She teaches City & Guilds embroidery both in the UK and the USA, lectures and teaches in Adult Education, and is the author of *Machine Embroidery* and *Fairy Tale Quilts and Embroidery* (both published by Merehurst). She is currently working on a new book on machine embroidery (to be published by B.T. Batsford).

Sarah Burgess teaches Embroidery and Surface Pattern at Sheffield College. She is an exhibiting member of several textile groups, and has shown her work - which explores the illusionary qualities of three-dimensional pattern, often developed from studies of architecture - in the UK, France, the USA and Japan. She has had several articles published in *The World of Embroidery*.

Margaret Charlton is a retired doctor who holds City & Guilds Parts I and II, and is a founder member of the Computer Textile Design Group, of which she is the Secretary. She specializes in using automatic patterns on the sewing machine to create rich fabrics. She has had articles published in *The World of Embroidery*.

Siân Martin, B.A. Hons, trained at the Birmingham College of Art, and holds a Master of Arts Degree in Embroidery. She belongs to the '62 Group and the New Fibre Art Group, and has frequently exhibited with them. She has taught at schools and colleges since gaining her Art Teachers' Diploma, and now teaches City & Guilds embroidery at three colleges. She is also the author and tutor of the City & Guilds Embroidery Correspondence Course, which many students from around the world have joined. She has had articles published in *The World of Embroidery*.

Heather Marsh is an embroiderer who specializes in making fine, soft felts from luxury fibres, which

Valerie Campbell-Harding   *Gail Harker*

Sarah Burgess   *Margaret Charlton*

Siân Martin   *Heather Marsh*   *Ruth Issett*

she dyes, stitches, pleats and pieces together to produce a variety of unusual manipulated surfaces. She teaches in Adult Education and has exhibited her work in the UK and abroad. She has had several articles published in *The World of Embroidery*.

Ruth Issett, B.A. Hons, has been a practising textile artist for over twenty years, and is a lecturer in adult education in Kent. Fascinated by all areas of printing, dyeing and embroidery, she likes to work using a combination of all three. She has had articles published in *The World of Embroidery*.

Maggie Grey, having completed City & Guilds Parts I and II, now spends most of her time teaching textile design on the computer and translating it into embroidery, worked both by hand and machine. She has had articles published in *The World of Embroidery* and holds workshops all over the country.

Julie Smith holds City & Guilds Parts I and II and L.C.G.I. She trained originally as a chemist and microbiologist, but now teaches City & Guilds

embroidery and City & Guilds patchwork at a number of different centres. She has exhibited her work widely in the UK. She has had several articles published in *The World of Embroidery*.

Pamela Watts has taught City & Guilds embroidery, is currently teaching City & Guilds patchwork and quilting, and is a Verifier for City and Guilds courses. She lectures and holds workshops all over the UK, and has had articles published in *The World of Embroidery*. She is the author of *Machine Embroidery: New Ideas and Techniques*, and co-author with Valerie Campbell-Harding of *Machine Embroidery: Stitch Techniques* and *Bead Embroidery* (all published by B.T. Batsford).

Mollie Picken, N.D.D., A.T.C., trained at Goldsmith's Art College in London, and has taught art in secondary schools, in Further Education Colleges and at Art Colleges. She is a member of the Society of Designer Craftsmen, and has exhibited her embroidery in the UK. Her illustrations have been published in 12 books, and are also sold as cards.

Maggie Grey   *Julie Smith*   *Pamela Watts*   *Mollie Picken*

INTRODUCTION

The idea for this book was born at the Embroiderers' Guild at Hampton Court Palace ,which has published several books inspired by its historic embroidery collection. It was suggested that the Guild's magazine, The World of Embroidery, should   offer 'how-to-do-it' books, containing projects designed by skilled embroiderers with an art training who would offer more in the way of expertise than is often found in project-based books.

This book – the result of that idea – is aimed at embroiderers who would like to make something rather more personal than they are offered in kit form, but who lack confidence in their ability to design and carry out a finished piece of work without help. The projects described here give full step-by-step instructions, but also suggest possible variations in colour schemes, types of thread and stitches to use, or small changes in the pattern or the design, which will help to make the embroidery just that bit different. Indeed, all the projects can be adapted in various ways, or can simply be used as sources of inspiration and as starting points for other designs. It can be great fun making these decisions, and means that a favourite project can be repeated in a new way, for another purpose.

A broad range of projects is included here, and the different working methods called for will appeal to embroiderers of all levels. The designs are planned to be simple, making effective use of materials and techniques, in glorious colours, with all the seduction of stitched textiles which one longs to touch. Some of the embroideries can be completed relatively quickly, while others are more ambitious in terms of the work involved, and will take longer.

The first part of the book includes information on the materials that will be needed to work the projects. There is an enormous variety of materials available today, which makes for confusing shopping, and some of the choices have been narrowed down so as to give guidance on which items to buy and how to use them. A section on techniques also explains, clearly and simply, various working methods used in the projects, such as enlarging or reducing a design and transferring it to fabric, colouring fabric, and working different stitches.

Each of the projects offers a straightforward, almost 'no-visible-design' approach, along with suggested colour schemes and ways to carry out the designs using simple embroidery techniques. The methods used have deliberately been chosen because they are capable of greater variation, and can therefore be adapted to make the embroideries more personal than difficult stitches or methods. The finished pieces, which range from book covers and cushions to a wallhanging and an eye-catching jacket, are practical as well as beautiful, and are ideal for use in the home or to give as personal and original gifts to family and friends.

The final section reveals how to make a wonderful array of cords, tassels and other embellishments. All are very simple to make, and will not only finish an embroidery beautifully, but also add the vital finishing touch that will produce a special piece of work.

The contributors to this book are all highly skilled embroiderers and tutors, and their clear designs and instructions, born of years of experience, will help you to be certain of success when tackling any of the projects. All the contributors have written magazine articles on embroidery subjects, some are authors of books on a variety of design and related topics, all are members of the Embroiderers' Guild. They teach beginners as well as more experienced students in Adult Education, some are Art College tutors, and some hold workshops for members of the Embroiderers' Guild or other groups both in Britain and abroad. They frequently exhibit their work, proving that they are practising embroiderers who understand the problems that may arise when undertaking a piece of work.

We hope that you will enjoy embroidering the projects included here, and that doing so will give you the confidence to launch out on your own designs – however simple – and to choose your own materials, stitches and techniques as you gain experience in the wonderful art of embroidery.

Valerie Campbell-Harding
Editor

MATERIALS
AND
TECHNIQUES

Gail Harker

*The materials needed for the projects in
this book are quite straightforward, but
choosing the right ones at the start will
help you to work quickly and easily.
The basic techniques are also explained,
and can be used as a source of reference as
you work on the projects.*

A selection of brightly coloured, contrasting fabrics. These were used for the 'Book cover' project on page 48.

FABRICS FOR EMBROIDERY

Almost any fabric may be used for embroidery, the main consideration being that it is suitable to support the weight of thread used. Many soft-furnishing fabrics, and traditional cotton, linen and some dressmaking fabrics, are suitable, as are some wool and synthetic blends.

The projects shown throughout the book will call for several different types of fabric. Most can be found in all shops selling fabrics, but some may only be found in bridal departments, or at shops specializing in embroidery materials or fabrics normally used for furnishings. If a specific fabric is called for in any of the projects that you are unable to find, choose a substitute with a similar weight and texture.

Cold-water-soluble fabric

This looks rather like plastic wrap and, as with other non-woven fabrics, is manufactured under different trade names. It is used by embroiderers for a number of techniques, in both hand and machine embroidery, and is suitable for machine stitching. A ball-point machine needle is generally the choice for stitching into this fabric by machine.

Cold-water-soluble fabric is suggested for trapping layers of fleece together, in preparation for felting, in the wallhanging project on page 80 – a running stitch is applied by hand to secure the layers. The fabric is then dissolved in the water used to felt the wool. If a specific design is being created, it is important to ensure that the stitches are interlocked across the whole piece. This 'grid' (geometric or not) holds the design elements in position when the backing is dissolved. When all the stitching has been applied, the fabric is dipped into cold water and dissolves, leaving behind the stitching. Hot-water-soluble fabric is also available and works in the same way, except that, as the name implies, hot water is used – follow the manufacturer's instructions.

Interfacing fabrics

These fabrics are available in a range of weights, from very light to very heavy, and can have stitching applied directly to them. Some interfacings, known as iron-on (fusible) interfacings, have a bonding surface on one side of the fabric which allows them to be fused to another fabric through the applied heat of an iron – be sure to read the manufacturer's instructions before use. Iron-on (fusible) interfacing is used as a backing for woven ribbons in the pansy-bags project on page 34. When interfacing is fused or sewn on to fabric, the combined materials create a greater weight or stiffness, allowing more stitching on a fabric which might otherwise be too light in weight.

Natural-fibre fabrics

The natural fabrics – cotton, silk and wool – are generally easier to handle and therefore more suitable for hand stitching than synthetic fabrics. Many of the projects in the book use natural fabrics, such as the plain-weave cotton suggested for the cushion on page 58, or habotai silk, which is used as a lining for one of the pansy bags on page 34 and the wall hanging on page 80. This silk is a soft, lightweight and relatively inexpensive fabric which takes dye well; it is ideal for any embroidery requiring colouration. It is also available ready-dyed in a wide range of colours.

Cotton muslin, another natural-fibre fabric, is a loosely woven lightweight fabric which is used as a backing. The quilted jacket on page 68 and cushion on page 102 both use muslin as the backing behind the wadding (batting) to complete the fabric 'sandwich'. Mull, a fabric similar in appearance to muslin, makes a satisfactory substitute.

Non-woven fabrics

These fabrics do not fray and they may be worked in any direction. Fabrics in this category include felt, leather and some synthetics. In the flowerpots project on page 94, gold kid (goatskin) is suggested as an alternative for the appliqué, as it is very thin, supple and easy to work. This hide may be a little difficult to find, but should be stocked by specialist suppliers.

PELMET VILENE

Pelmet Vilene (also sold under different names) is the heaviest of the non-woven fabrics. It was developed for use in the making of soft furnishings such as curtain headings, and is available in both narrow and wide widths. It is intended to provide maximum fabric stiffness, and is used for this reason in the book-covers project on page 48. Pelmet Vilene is very adaptable – it dyes well, accepts fabric paints, and may be used unframed for machine embroidery and with automatic machine stitches. A #90 or #100 machine needle should be used with this type of fabric.

A detail of the tassel cushion on page 63

A detail of the book cover on page 55

Ribbons

Ribbons are made today in a huge variety of widths, fabrics, patterns, colours and finishes. They are widely available in department stores and by mail order, and most types can be used for embroidery. Resist the temptation to use florist's (paper) ribbon, however, unless it will hold up to stitching and is to be used on an item which will not require washing.

If you cannot find the exact ribbon you want, be creative and make your own. Cut up any fabric into strips, turn under the edges, and use as required. This can be a little time-consuming, but is well worth the effort to achieve the right effect. Home-cut strips may be used for stitching or as a direct substitute for the ribbons used in the pansy-bags project on page 34. The ribbons and strips are bonded on to iron-on (fusible) interfacing to make a 'fabric'.

Lightweight fabrics are easily torn into strips by making a small cut on the fabric at the desired width. Tear with both hands along the grain of the fabric. If the fabric frays more than is acceptable, either choose a different type of fabric or cut the strips rather than tearing them. A good way of cutting strips accurately and evenly is to lay the fabric over a cutting mat or board, align a straight edge at the desired width with a metal ruler (not a plastic one) and then to cut using a rotary knife. Alternatively, you can mark the fabric with a disappearing fabric marker and then carefully cut the strips using a pair of sharp sewing scissors.

Transparent fabrics

Lightweight, diaphanous fabrics are often used to create dimensional effects in embroidery, as well as adding extra colour, and are suggested for use in the book-cover and flowerpot projects on pages 48 and 94 respectively.

Organza is a transparent fabric that is frequently used for embroidery. Silk organza has a shiny appearance with a crisp texture. It accepts dyes and paints well and has a lovely sewing quality. Nylon organza is available in a wide range of colours and weights. It was first made to simulate silk organza, and has most of the same qualities. A layer of organza is also used between the wadding (batting) and the black top fabric for the quilted jacket on page 68, to prevent the white of the wadding (batting) from showing through.

Alternatives to organza include cotton organdie, which is slightly less transparent than organza, and frays less easily. It

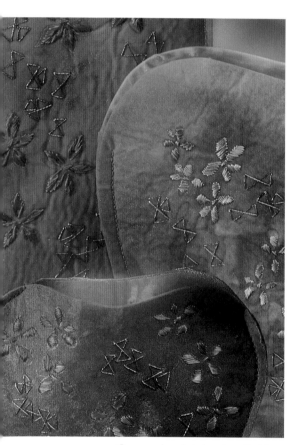

Organza is painted and applied to a pelmet vilene base. Embroidery is then worked over the surface, (see 'Flower pots' on page 94)

also has a crisper texture. Silk chiffon is a very thin, sheer fabric which frays easily. The fraying aspect may, however, be used to advantage for some projects.

Vilene Bondaweb (Fusible webbing)

This product (also sold under different names) is very useful for applying one fabric to another. It is covered by backing paper to allow separate bonding to each side, so that a 'sandwich' of fabrics can be made with the Bondaweb (fusible webbing) in the middle. Applied pieces may be large or small, although pieces greater than 50 cm (20 in) in any direction could cause problems as a result of uneven heat application, creating an unwanted bubble effect, although this could, of course, be desirable as a texture for some work. The flowerpots on page 94 and the book covers on page 48 both use Bondaweb (fusible webbing) to appliqué small fabric pieces to the background.

As with iron-on (fusible) interfacing, always read the manufacturer's instructions before use, as this product can vary and may require a slightly different process. It is also always advisable to test a small sample before committing to the finished piece, as fabrics may react in unexpected ways.

Wadding (Batting)

Both the jacket on page 68 and the cushion on page 102 use wadding (batting) to give a feeling of depth to the quilting. Various types are available, ranging from thick to thin, in natural or synthetic fibres. Choose the thickness, or weight, of wadding (batting) to suit the project in hand, bearing in mind that, if it is very thick, items will be stiff and difficult to stitch without causing puckering.

Use polyester wadding (batting) for items that will need to be washed, as this is durable and washable, whereas cotton wadding has a tendency to shrink. Silk wadding requires care and should not be washed frequently, but is extremely light in weight. For machine quilting, the thinnest and lightest types of wadding (batting) are the easiest to work.

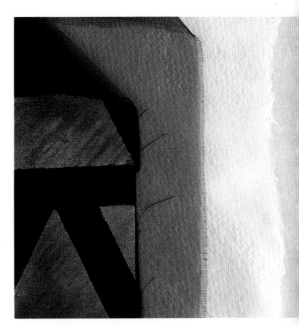

Here wadding is used in a quilted jacket which is coloured with fabric paint sticks, (see page 68)

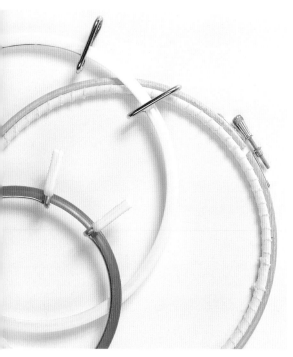

A selection of ring frames

EMBROIDERY FRAMES

Historically, embroidery was almost always worked in the hand, with frames rarely being used except for goldwork, which is still the case today. In the East, pieces of work were sometimes held taut by being pinned to the worker's trouser knee, or to a small, heavy cushion (similar to a pincushion) in a metal frame which was clamped to a table.

Although frames are not specified for the projects in this book, you may prefer to use one if you find that it makes the stitching easier to do or the work more comfortable to hold. Canvaswork (tapestry) and some machine embroidery are better done in a frame to avoid too much distortion, for instance, although it is easier to work some stitches, such as chain stitch (which needs three 'stabs' to make each stitch), in the hand.

If you do intend to use a frame, it is best to use a wooden ring frame. Place the outer ring on a table or work surface, position the fabric over it, and then press the inner (bound) ring down into it. Partially tighten the screw by hand, then gently pull the fabric taut, working all round the ring. Finally, tighten the screw fully with a screwdriver. An alternative to a wooden ring frame is a modern spring frame, which, although it does not hold the fabric taut all over, is quite adequate for stitching small areas.

Binding a frame

Embroidery frames can be covered with bias binding before use to protect the embroidery being worked. To do this, take a length of bias binding and open out the fold. Glue one end of the binding to the inner ring of the frame, holding the bias at a 45° angle. When the glue is dry, wrap the bias round the ring, overlapping each row slightly to hide the previous raw edge, and moving forward as you wrap. When you arrive back at the starting point, fold over the edge of the bias and sew it to the bound ring, on the inside so that it does not create extra bulk between it and the outer ring.

THREADS FOR HAND EMBROIDERY

Threads are manufactured from a range of fibres: cotton, silk, wool, linen, synthetics (such as rayon and polyester) and metal. Cotton, wool and polyester threads are the most readily available, and are made in the widest variety of colours.

It is important to consider the effect you are trying to achieve in a piece of work when choosing threads for embroidery, as each type of thread has individual characteristics and will affect the look of the finished embroidery. For this reason, trying different types as well as colours of thread in a needle simultaneously can produce a range of exciting – and sometimes unexpected – textures and finishes.

Another factor in selecting threads is the purpose for which the thread is needed – for instance, whether it is to be purely decorative or whether it needs to be fairly strong. Dressmaking threads are generally made of twisted cotton or polyester, or cotton-wrapped polyester. All three are strong, and are therefore used for sewing seams and for making up garments of all kinds. Buttonhole thread is even stronger, and may be useful for items which need to be very hardwearing. Another practical aspect – whether the finished item will need to be laundered or cleaned frequently – must also be taken into account. Care and cleaning information will be supplied by the thread manufacturer, and should be noted before purchase.

A final consideration is the 'user-friendliness' of the threads. Some metallic threads, for example, can be fairly difficult to use and may therefore be best avoided initially by newcomers to embroidery when another type of thread could be used in their place. The following embroidery threads are widely available and have a range of uses.

Coton à broder

This is a very lightly twisted, soft-looking, single cotton thread, and has some sheen to its surface.

Cotton perle (pearl cotton)

This is a mercerized cotton thread with a very shiny finish. It is also supplied in skeins, but has a more pronounced twist than six-stranded cotton and cannot be split. It produces an embossed effect when stitched.

Crewel wool (yarn)

This 2-ply thread consists of fine, twisted wool (yarn). It is most often used in crewel and canvaswork (tapestry), as well as for other stitching such as embroidery.

Knitting, weaving and crochet yarns
These have a variable fibre content and come in a range of thicknesses and colours. As well as the purposes for which they are produced, they can be used for embroidery.

Silk thread
Silk thread is available either stranded or twisted, and has a high sheen.

Six-stranded cotton
Also sometimes known as stranded floss, this is a lustrous, 100 per cent mercerized cotton thread made in about four hundred colours. It consists of lightly twisted strands which are supplied in skeins. These can be used as supplied, or the strands may be split into one or more threads before use.

Soft embroidery cotton
This is a fairly thick, 5-ply, soft cotton thread with a matt finish. It is a good choice for embroidery beginners.

Space-dyed thread
As the name suggests, this type of thread is specially dyed so that a single thread has many colours appearing irregularly spaced over the length of the thread. As a result, it creates a varied and wonderfully colourful appearance when worked. Space-dyed thread is available from specialist needlework shops and some department stores.

Tapestry wool (yarn)
This is made of twisted wool and has a matt finish. It is a fairly heavy 4-ply thread and cannot be split into individual strands.

Opposite *A selection of hand embroidery threads*

THREADS FOR MACHINE EMBROIDERY

Most threads are developed for specific purposes. Dressmaking threads, for instance, are manufactured with a high degree of twist which contributes to their strength and durability – factors which are obviously important when making garments which will undergo considerable stress. The high twist means, however, that, when they are applied, these threads do not spread and show off their colour and lustre. Threads made for machine embroidery are not subjected to the high twist and are therefore less strong, but spread beautifully on fabric as they are applied, revealing their lovely colour and sheen.

These threads are supplied by a number of manufacturers in a wide range of fibres, including cotton, silk, rayon, polyester, metallics, or blends of several fibres. They are usually also supplied in different sizes, from #50 (very thin) to #30 (thick). (You will find that some threads are unnumbered, however.) When using the heavier or thicker threads, and also metallics, try using a #90 or, perhaps, a #100 needle size, as this will make the stitching easier. It may also be helpful to reduce your machine's top tension slightly. Almost any ordinary thread may be used in the bobbin for machine embroidery, as long as the back of the fabric will not be seen. If it will be seen, the colour and type of bobbin thread used should also be taken into account to produce an attractive finish.

It is always advisable to test threads for suitability before using them for a project. This takes very little time – simply work a small sample of stitches on a spare piece of fabric. Testing threads in this way is always worth the effort and may save a lot of time, as it will tell you whether your machine is able to handle the thread and stitches, without spoiling a half-finished piece of work.

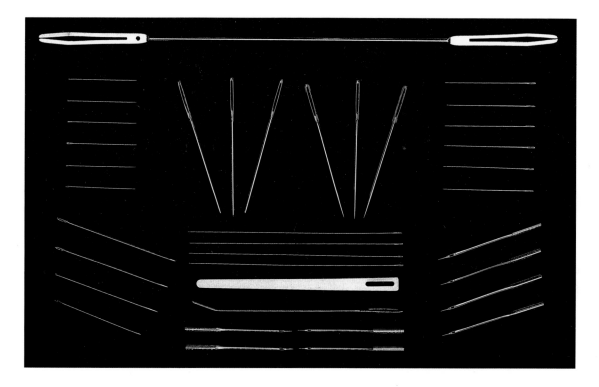

Hand and machine needles

NEEDLES FOR HAND STITCHING

There are numerous types of needle on the market. Each type is available in a range of sizes, classified by gauge (diameter), length and the size of the eye. The largest needles are identified by the smallest numbers, while the smallest needles have the largest numbers. If your chosen thread does not pass easily through the eye of a needle, use a needle with a larger eye, so as not to damage the thread. Conversely, you may prefer to use a needle with a large eye for ease of threading, but, if the needle makes too large a hole or distorts the fabric, choose another one. If you find threading a needle difficult, use a needle threader or, cut a narrow strip of paper, fold it in half, place the thread in the fold and pull it through the eye. Trimming the thread end with sharp scissors will also help. The following types of needle are all useful:

Beading
A very long, thin needle, specifically designed for threading beads.

21

Between/Quilting

This has a sharp point and is ideal for short, quick, even stitching, making it invaluable for quilters.

Bodkin

Although not technically a needle, this falls into the same category. It has a blunt point and may be flat or round with a large eye for threading cord or elastic. It is also used for darning.

Chenille

This needle has a sharp point and large eye, and is good for stitching thick yarns on to coarse fabrics.

Crewel/Embroidery

These have a sharp point, with a long eye to facilitate the passing of one or more threads through it. This is the most commonly used needle for most types of surface embroidery.

Darning

This large needle has a sharp point and may be used for stitching thick fabrics.

Sharps

These have a sharp point and are used for sewing, patchwork, quilting and the making up of garments and other items.

Tapestry

This has a blunt, rounded point with a large, long eye to accommodate wool and heavier yarns. It is designed to slip between threads rather than splitting them. A tapestry needle is good for use on even and plain-weave fabrics – for example, those used for canvaswork (tapestry), cross stitch and darning.

NEEDLES FOR MACHINE STITCHING

Charts supplied by manufacturers which specify needle size versus thread size are not directly applicable to machine embroidery. Quite often, for instance, a heavier needle than that recommended will be required to accommodate threads of blended fibres or even of twisted metallics. Such charts should therefore only be used as a rough guide.

CONTINENTAL AND UK NEEDLE SIZES

UK	8	9	10	11	12	14	16	18	20
Continental	60	65	70	75	80	90	100	110	120
	VERY FINE			MEDIUM			VERY HEAVY		

A medium-sized (UK 14, Continental 90) needle is a good choice for beginners to machine embroidery, when using a medium-weight fabric. It is more resistant to flexing and bending than a finer needle and is, as a result, more tolerant of unpractised hand movements. Fine needles are easily bent, and can miss stitches or break and shred threads when working on very heavy fabrics. The following three are useful:

Ballpoint
Synthetic fabrics and knits can resist a sharp-pointed needle and cause skipped stitches. A ballpoint needle helps to overcome these problems, as it tends to push fibres aside while stitching, rather than piercing and splitting them (rather as a tapestry needle does when hand stitching). A ballpoint needle is also very effective on soluble fabrics.

Jeans
This needle is designed to pierce very stiff, dense fabric, and has a very sharp and tapered point. It is excellent for stitching on heavy fabrics and also works well on interfacings.

Topstitch
This has a special design with a larger-than-normal eye. It is used for automatic and free machine embroidery, and is very helpful in accommodating heavy threads and other difficult

ENLARGING OR REDUCING A DESIGN
One of the first steps in the creation of any piece of needlework is the development of a design. It is generally desirable to make a design to the size of the finished piece, but, where the finished item is to be either very large or very small, this may be impractical, and enlargement or reduction of the design may be needed.

It is important to be aware that the appearance of a design can change radically as it is scaled up or down in size. A design can look very sparse when it is enlarged, while much of the detail can be 'lost' through reduction. It is important, therefore, to produce the design to its actual size before proceeding with scaling it up or down.

Using a photocopier

There are a number of practical ways to enlarge or reduce a design – one of the easiest is by using a photocopier. Most ordinary office photocopiers will make copies of up to 42 x 30 cm (16 ½ x 11 ¾ in), or A3 size. If the finished design is larger than the largest-size paper available on the machine, you will need to enlarge the design in sections first and then carefully piece them together.

Many photocopiers will be capable of enlarging or reducing a design to a percentage of the actual size of the original. The percentage of enlargement or reduction is easily calculated using the following method. Measure the length of the original artwork, then establish the desired length of the related side of the finished piece. Divide the length of the original artwork into the desired length of the finished piece – the resultant number will be the number of times the design must be enlarged or reduced in order to achieve the finished size. Multiply this by one hundred, and this will be the percentage of enlargement or reduction.

Set the photocopier to the calculated percentage and make the copy. If the copier will not accept a large or small enough percentage, you may need to complete the process in two more steps. As an example:

Length of original artwork = 12.5 cm (5 in)
Length of finished piece = 50 cm (20 in)
50 (20) ÷ 12.5 (5) = 4
4 x 100 = 400% enlargement

Most photocopiers will not accommodate such a large percentage in one step. If this is the case, a 100% enlargement will double the size of the original. Take the enlarged photocopy and enlarge that a further 100% to achieve the required 400% enlargement. Reverse the process to make a similar reduction of a design if necessary.

TRANSFERRING A DESIGN TO FABRIC

Once you have completed your design, you will need to transfer it to the fabric. A number of products are available for this purpose, of which the three most useful are described below.

Air-soluble felt-tip marker

This type of marker makes a line – generally blue or purple – which fades from view after about twenty-four hours. Different markers vary in performance depending on the manufacturer and the type of fabric used, so always make a trial sample before marking the main piece of fabric.

Tailor's or dressmaker's chalk

This is often made in the form of a normal writing pencil, or as a wedge of chalk-like material with thin edges which are used for marking the fabric. It generally comes in an off-white or yellow colour, and is therefore more visible when used on dark than on lighter fabrics. The marking medium can be brushed off the fabric once the design has been stitched (the pencil variety often comes with a small brush at the top end for this purpose).

Water-soluble felt-tip marker

This type of marker can be used to draw a design directly on to fabric, which is then erased after stitching. Some types of marker have one end as the drawing point, and the other end as the 'eraser'. If it has only the marking tip, use a cotton bud (swab), moistened with water, to remove the lines. Always test this type of marker on a spare piece of fabric before use.

COLOURING FABRIC

Applying colour to fabric through painting and printing can produce some vivid creative effects, and a wide range of colouring products is available, some of which are described below. The colour may be applied before any stitching begins to create wonderful patterned backgrounds for embroidery. Different techniques are required for each product, but, before using any of them, you must first wash the fabric in a mild detergent to remove all sizing and finishing materials which could interfere with the fabric's ability to accept the paint or dye. Allow the fabric to dry, then press to remove any creases.

Paints, crayons and paint sticks can be used to colour fabrics and enhance existing designs.

Markal Paint Sticks

These paint sticks, used in the jacket project on page 68, consist of oil-based pigments moulded into chubby crayons. They are available in a wide variety of colours, as well as in metallic and iridescent mixtures.

To use the paint sticks, first tape the washed and pressed fabric to a table or work surface with masking tape so that it is taut and will not move about. Apply the colours, either using the paint sticks as crayons in the ordinary way, or brushing on colour to create an interesting texture. Allow the paint to 'cure' for a minimum of forty-eight hours before heat-setting both sides of the fabric with the hottest dry iron that your fabric will tolerate. Refer to the manufacturer's instructions before committing the whole piece to any washing or dry-cleaning process and, if possible, test a spare piece of coloured fabric first to be certain of good results.

Multi-purpose fabric paints

Many dyes are held in an emulsion-type base and are often called fabric paints. The creamy consistency makes the paints easy to work, and colours may be heat-set (using an iron) for washability once the fabric has dried. Good makes of fabric paint include Dylon Colour Fun, Pebeo Seta Colour and Deka Permanent (all available from craft suppliers – see the list of Suppliers on page 124). These work particularly well on interfacings as well as on many other types of fabric. The pansy-bag project on page 35 describes how to make a printing block for the application of the paint. Refer to the manufacturer's instructions on heat-setting the paints, as these may vary slightly with different makes.

Silk paints

Silk paints are too thin for printing on to fabric, but can be used to create a variety of painted effects, from all-over, even colourings to interesting mottled or spattered textures. It is also possible to co-ordinate fabric colours for projects such as the book covers on page 49 using silk paints. Most natural fabrics and some synthetics can be coloured using this method, and will take the paints well.

Many varieties of silk paints are now on the market, the most readily available being the water-soluble variety, which are simple to use at home. The main requirement is a clear expanse of table, work surface or floor on which to work and

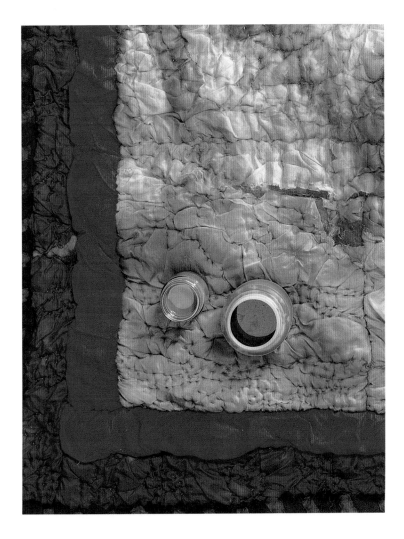

Silk paints are used to colour the silk fabric on the back of the wall hanging, which can be seen on page 92.

where the fabric can be left to dry. You will also need jars of clean water, a paintbrush or small pieces of sponge, and of course the paints in colours of your choice.

Lay down a large piece of plastic sheeting or other non-absorbent water-containing material on the surface. This will not only protect the surface, but will also be instrumental in achieving certain mottled effects. Lay the washed and ironed fabric on the prepared surface and tape it down with masking tape so that it is taut. Spray or dip heavy fabrics and interfacings in water before applying colour, then squeeze them out and lay on the surface.

Prepare the paints by mixing them with a little water, referring to the manufacturer's instructions. The paints should have a fairly watery consistency, although bear in mind that the more water you add, the paler the colours will be. Brush or sponge the colours on to the fabric, rinsing the brush before using each new colour, and avoiding over-saturation of very thin fabrics. Interfacings may require more persuasion in accepting colours – force additional colour into non-receptive areas with the brush or a sponge.

Leave the fabric undisturbed to dry overnight (silks and other light fabrics may dry in a few hours). You can use a hairdryer to accelerate the drying time, but this has a tendency to halt the attractive mottled effects created when the fabric is left to dry naturally. If you do use a hairdryer, avoid spot-heating of sensitive fabrics such as silk.

When the fabric is completely dry, set or 'fix' the paints, always referring to the manufacturer's instructions. Most silk paints may be set using an iron, but be sure to use a pressing cloth over delicate fabrics. After setting, most fabrics will be colourfast in washing conditions usual for the fabric.

Transfer crayons

These can be used to produce bright, vivid colours on a range of fabrics. Most manufacturers recommend the crayons for use on synthetic fabrics, which take the colours particularly well, but do always check the instructions supplied. The coloured fabric is generally washable in warm water. Colours may be applied one or more at a time, and may be laid over each other to create blends and tones (this technique is used very effectively in the cushion project on page 103).

To use transfer crayons, first work the design on a sheet of white paper. Apply the colours to the paper, following your design, then lay the paper, coloured-side down, on to the washed and pressed fabric. To transfer the design from the paper to the fabric, place a pressing cloth over the paper, then press with a hot, dry iron. Avoid running the iron over the paper – simply press, lift and press again until you have covered the whole area. You can check whether the design has been transferred properly by carefully lifting a corner of the paper and looking underneath. Transfers may be used up to five times, – the colour will obviously diminish with each application, but this can create an attractive effect.

HAND STITCHES

Back stitch

From the front, this resembles an interlocking machine stitch. Each stitch should be exactly the same length. To work back stitch, bring the needle up from the wrong side of the fabric at a point just beyond the starting point of the stitching line. Bring the needle back to the starting point of the stitching line and take it to the wrong side of the fabric, bringing it up again just beyond the first point. This will leave a stitch-length space. Once again, take the needle back, across the space, and take it to the wrong side of the fabric.

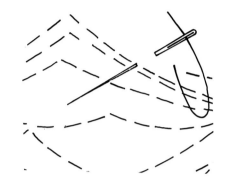

Eyelet

This is used for the book covers on page 49. Trace or draw the outline of a circle on the fabric. Using small, sharp scissors, carefully cut around the circumference and remove the circle. Work buttonhole stitch evenly around the edge to create a decorative effect. The fabric is fused on to Vilene Bondaweb (fusible webbing), the qualities of which reduce fraying problems when the central circles are cut out.

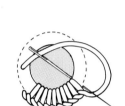

Herringbone stitch

This stitch is used for the torn-fabric-weave pansy bag on page 36. Work from left to right between horizontal parallel lines, first bringing the needle through the bottom line. Take the thread diagonally to the top line, taking a small stitch (work the needle from right to left). Angle the thread diagonally towards the bottom line, crossing the first thread and taking another small stitch on the bottom line. The resulting crossed threads make one complete stitch. Take care as you work not to loop the thread as in buttonhole stitch. As a variation, try working a second colour over the first pattern.

Running stitch

This is one of the easiest and most basic of embroidery stitches, accomplished through a simple in-and-out movement of the needle through the fabric. The stitches should have small spaces between them. These could be uniform, or variable in size for added interest. Running stitch may be used on all types of fabric with almost any thread. It is used for the cushion on page 59 and the flowerpots on page 95. Try also using whipped running stitch (see overleaf) as a variation.

Satin stitch

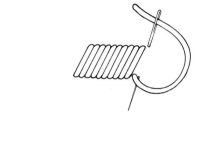

Satin stitch consists of parallel stitches closely worked to form a 'solid' stitched shape. It is used for the flowerpots on page 94. Draw flower shapes as guidelines, then angle the stitches across the petal shapes, each in a slightly different direction to create a play of light on the sheen of the thread.

Slip stitch

This simple stitch is used for a number of the projects and is particularly useful for appliqué and project construction. When the stitch is properly worked, it should be almost invisible. With a threaded needle, pick up a very small amount of background fabric. Slip the needle into the edge of the piece to be applied, again taking as little fabric as possible, and then take the needle back into the background fabric.

Twisted chain stitch

Twisted chain stitch has a highly textured appearance. Work the stitch from the top down. Using a vertical guideline, bring the needle from the wrong to the right side of the fabric at the top of the line. Hold the working thread down with your left thumb, forming the thread in a loop. Take the needle in and out of the fabric at a slight angle along the guideline, not in the previous entry holes but just off to the side. Release the loop and draw through the thread. (In simple chain stitch, the loop always begins and ends in the same needle-insertion point, rather than just off to the side.) Twisted chain stitch is used for the cushion on page 103.

Whipped running stitch

This is a simple variation on ordinary running stitch, and is used for the cushion on page 58. First work a row of even running stitches. When the row is complete, work over the tops of the stitches, using the first row as a basis for the whipped stitches. Work the whipped stitch across the running stitches, passing over and over the thread. Be careful that you do not pick up any background fabric while working whipped running stitch.

MACHINE EMBROIDERY

Our modern industrial society has placed at our disposal hundreds of domestic sewing machines manufactured in all parts of the world. These machines vary enormously in price, and, as a general rule, the more expensive the machine, the more capabilities or 'functions' it will have. The more sophisticated models may even be computerized. However, even the most humble electric sewing machine will be suitable for working the projects contained in this book, and will provide you with some interesting patterns.

Automatic stitches and patterns

Automatic stitches are worked with the presser foot attached to the machine, and consist of those stitches which are accessed through a pressed button, insertion of a cam, or through a computer-screen selection. Some manufacturers label these stitches as 'utility' or 'decorative' stitches, especially if they are basically designed for a specific function. A special foot is sometimes provided for these stitches. The most basic of machines will almost always provide a few stitch options, such as straight stitch and zigzag or satin stitch – in all cases, read your machine manual to familiarize yourself with your particular machine's capabilities and limitations.

When working automatic stitches, it is important to support dense stitching with a backing fabric such as interfacing. Heavy interfacing is an easy surface to stitch on and can also be used alone.

Be alert to all the possibilities available to you while stitching. You can vary stitches while you work by simply changing the length or width of the stitch you are using. Changing the stitch length will cause stitches to sit further apart or closer together; altering the width will cause the stitching line to become wider or narrower.

Some of the projects may indicate a certain kind of patterned stitch. If your machine does not have a particular stitch, use another, similar one. Try out all the available stitches before starting on a project, so that you know what you can do and which stitches work well on which types of fabric. It is best to use machine-embroidery thread for working automatic patterns, as some of the patterns may cause machine stoppage if the thread is too heavy.

Machine preparation

Ensure that the top thread and bobbin thread are in balance – that is, that the two threads lock in the centre of the fabric you are stitching. You can test this by using different thread colours for the top and bottom – sew a few stitches and check to see that the bobbin-thread colour does not show on the top

Different stitch patterns and thread colours are used to create a rich, textured effect, (see the 'Book covers' on page 49).

of the fabric, then turn the fabric over and check that the top thread is not showing on the reverse side.

If the bobbin thread shows on the top of the fabric, either of two remedies are possible. The first option, which should always be tried first, is to reduce the top tension; the second is gradually to increase the bobbin tension until the bobbin thread is no longer visible on the top of the fabric.

Most sewing machines have a top-tension indicator dial with a knob or lever with which to make adjustments. The scale will generally run from 0 to 10 (for most of your usual sewing, the dial will probably rest between 4 and 5). Reducing the top tension will mean reducing the number setting to a lower number. Some machines, however, merely indicate the top tension as a plus (+) or minus (-) symbol. In this case, a reduction in tension means moving in the direction of the minus (-) sign.

If you have balanced a thread tension for straight stitch, you will often need to adjust it a little when you came to work zigzag stitch or other automatic patterns. If so, adjust the tension as above. It does not really matter if the top thread shows slightly on the underside of the fabric, unless both sides will be visible on the finished item.

Machine quilting with straight stitch

If you intend to quilt by machine, it is most important that you have first tacked (basted) the 'sandwich' of fabric together securely and removed all the pins. If your machine is supplied with a walking foot (a top-feed device), this will help to feed the layers evenly through the machine. It is a good idea to work a sample piece of quilting first, using the same fabric, wadding (batting) and threads as those selected for the work. The jacket on page 76 is quilted, and this could be undertaken by hand or machine.

Dressmaker's threads are strong and are a good choice for quilting if the finished piece needs to be very hardwearing. Machine-embroidery threads are less strong but are more lustrous, and could be used where strength and durability are not paramount. Most sewing machines have a set stitch length of about 3 mm (⅛ in). Your test piece will demonstrate whether or not this is satisfactory for your work. Adjust the stitch length until no puckering of the fabric occurs while you stitch. You will often need a fairly long stitch to accommodate the extra thickness of the wadding (batting) and fabric layers.

A detail of the quilted jacket on page 76

PANSY BAGS

Sarah Burgess

These beautiful bags are created from woven strips of torn fabric and ribbons, embellished with stitchery. The wonderful colours would add a touch of flair to an elegant evening outfit – perhaps for a special occasion.

PANSY BAGS

The softly shaded blues, yellows and purples in a drift of pansies were the starting point for these delicate little bags. The idea developed from variations on a simple ribbon weave, and from experimentation using both strong contrasts and more subtle gradations of colour. Stitchery has been used to develop the designs further and to add an additional layer to the colour mix.

There are two sets of instructions for the two bags shown here. One design uses mainly strips of torn fabric, with a few ribbons. It is decorated completely by hand using traditional stitches, and has a hand-braided ribbon and thread strap. The second bag is made wholly of ribbons and is decorated using simple techniques on the sewing machine. It has a machine-stitched, twisted cord strap and is lined with silk which is hand-printed with a simple woven pattern.

The quantities and types of materials given here can be used if you wish to follow the designs exactly, but they can also be varied in almost innumerable ways. The ideas shown here should be just a starting point for your own imagination. Substituting your own colour scheme, is easy, provided that the number of fabrics and ribbons is the same as those given.

Another possibility would be to combine ideas from each of the designs, inter-mixing hand and machine stitchery. The woven-ribbon 'fabric' does not need to be confined to bags – it would make a wonderful cushion panel. You could even make a set of cushions in co-ordinating colours and varying designs to match the décor of a room.

TORN-FABRIC WEAVE

EQUIPMENT

Iron and ironing board

Clean towel or other soft ironing surface

Dressmaking pins

Piece of clean cotton fabric (for ironing)

Sharp sewing scissors

Sewing needle

Ruler

Water-soluble marker pen or tailor's chalk

Crewel needle

Tapestry needle

MATERIALS

(FOR THE BAG)

A selection of plain and/or patterned cotton and/or satin fabric in your chosen colours

21 x 21 cm (8 ½ x 8 ½in) medium-weight iron-on (fusible) interfacing

14 lengths of 25 cm x 13 mm (10 x ½ in) Offray sheer polyester ribbon: yellow, hunter, wine, royal, purple and torrid orange

Dressmaker's sewing thread for tacking (basting)

DMC cotton-perle thread no. 5: colours 741, 725, 3687 and 793

14 lengths of 25 cm x 3 mm (10 x ⅛ in) Offray

36

grosgrain and double-faced satin ribbon: mulberry, baby maize, smoke blue, orchid, chartreuse, apple green and yellow gold

(FOR THE STRAP — THESE MATERIALS WILL MAKE A LENGTH OF APPROXIMATELY 125 CM [50 IN])

6 m (8 yds) DMC cotton-perle thread no. 5: colours 741, 3687 and 793

3 m x 3 mm (4 yds x ⅛ in) Offray grosgrain ribbon: orchid and yellow gold

3 m x 3 mm (4 yds x ⅛ in) Offray double-faced satin ribbon: mulberry, baby maize, smoke blue, orchid, chartreuse and yellow gold

METHOD

TO MAKE THE BAG

1 Press your chosen fabrics; tear them along the grain into strips approximately 2 cm (¾ in) wide. You will need 24 strips in all, each 25 cm (10 in) in length. Press the torn strips again.

2 Place the square of iron-on (fusible) interfacing on the towel or other soft ironing surface, with the shiny (adhesive) side facing upward.

3 Lay 12 of the torn-fabric strips horizontally across the interfacing so that they cover the surface (see diagram overleaf). You can mix the colours randomly, or shade them from light to dark. Pin each strip into the towel or

Cotton and silk strips, and cotton perle thread, are used to make this pansy bag.

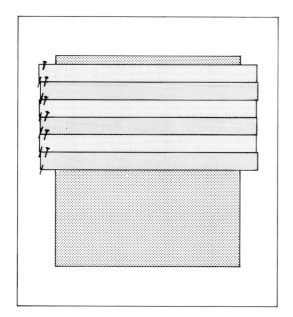

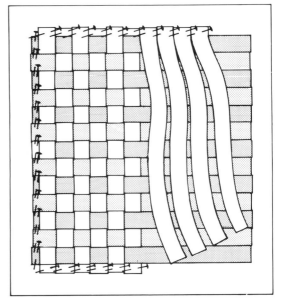

Lay strips of torn fabric or ribbons horizontally across iron-on (fusible) interfacing. Pin the strips into a towel or soft ironing surface on the left-hand side.

Lay vertical strips of torn fabric or ribbon across the horizontal strips and pin at the top. Weave the strips together, over and under. Pin on all sides.

soft ironing surface at the left-hand side, leaving the rest of the length free.

4 Lay the remaining 12 fabric strips on top of the horizontal strips, and pin them into the ironing surface at the top. Fold back the vertical fabric strips.

5 Take the first left-hand vertical strip and weave it under and then over the horizontal strips, pinning it straight at the bottom. Repeat with the next vertical strip, this time weaving over and then under the horizontal strips (see diagram above right). Pin it straight at the bottom.

6 Repeat this process with all the vertical strips to produce a woven 'fabric'. You may need to juggle the strips slightly once you have completed the weaving, to get them to lie flat and straight, with the interfacing completely hidden. Pin the fabric ends straight on all four sides.

7 Cover the weaving with the piece of cotton fabric and press firmly with a hot iron to bond the fabric strips to the interfacing. Be careful not to slide the iron over the surface,

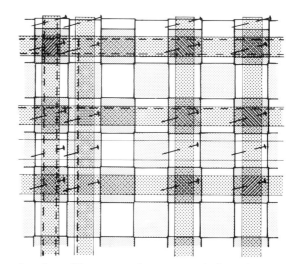

Lay sheer ribbons across the weave vertically and horizontally to blend the colours. Pin and tack (baste) in place (see step 8 on page 40).

Torn fabric bag *Fabric strips and ribbons are woven and decorated with embroidery. The ribbon and thread strap is braided and the tassel is made up using ribbons and threads.*

as this may disturb the weave – instead, apply the heat to one section, then lift the iron and move it to the next section, until you have covered the whole area. Remove all the pins, turn the weaving over carefully and iron again from the reverse, through the cotton fabric, to fix the strips thoroughly.

8 Pin and then tack (baste) the sheer ribbons vertically and horizontally across the right side of the weave (see diagram on page 38 [bottom]). The ribbon colours will mix beautifully where they overlap.

9 Use the ruler and marker pen or tailor's chalk to rule two lines approximately 5mm (¼ in) apart down the middle of the ribbons. Taking the crewel needle and a length of cotton perle, work a band of herringbone stitch or buttonhole stitch (see right) along the length of the ribbons, using the drawn lines as a guide. Change the colours as you wish. Remove the tacking (basting) threads.

10 Using the tapestry needle, thread a length of 3 mm (⅛ in) grosgrain or double-faced satin ribbons through the stitching and pin at either end. Repeat until you have used up all 14 lengths of ribbon. Stitch all the threaded ribbons firmly at either end to secure, and remove the pins.

Divide the threads and ribbons into three groups of two ribbons and two lengths of cotton perle, and braid the three groups together (see page 114).

TO MAKE THE TASSEL

The tassel can be added if desired. For this you will need 30 lengths of different coloured ribbons and a selection of cotton-perle threads. See method on page 117, adding the ribbons to the threads when you wrap them round the card.

To make up the bag follow the instructions on page 46, omitting Steps 6 and 7.

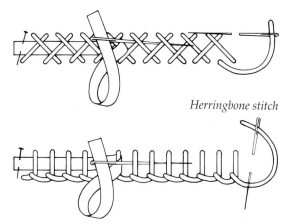

Herringbone stitch

Buttonhole stitch

TO MAKE THE STRAP

Tie together, at one end, a double length of the three cotton-perle threads and the single lengths of ribbon.

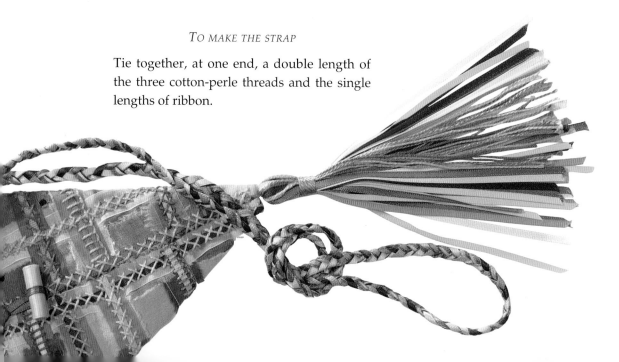

RIBBON WEAVE

EQUIPMENT

Sharp sewing scissors

Iron and ironing-board

Clean towel or other soft ironing surface

Dressmaking pins

Piece of clean cotton fabric (for ironing)

Tapestry needle

Sewing needle

Sewing machine

MATERIALS

(FOR THE BAG)

(Note: you can use your own combination of ribbons rather than those specified here, as long as the total number of ribbons of each width is the same.)

OFFRAY RIBBONS: GROUP A

3 lengths of 25 cm x 15 mm (10 x ¾ in) double-faced satin ribbon: grape and Royal

3 lengths of 25 cm x 23 mm (10 x 1 in) double-faced satin ribbon: yellow gold

25 cm x 5 mm (10 x ¼ in) feather-edged ribbon: lemon

2 lengths of 25 cm x 23 mm (10 x 1 in) grosgrain ribbon: antique blue, baby maize

25 cm x 23 mm (10 x 1 in) grosgrain ribbon: print blue

2 lengths of 25 cm x 15 mm (10 x ¾ in) grosgrain ribbon: regal purple

2 lengths of 25 cm x 9 mm (10 x ⅜ in) grosgrain ribbon: print blue

25 cm x 10 mm (10 x ½ in) velvet ribbon: green and yellow

25 cm x 13 mm (10 x ⅝ in) sheer ribbon: wine, yellow and purple

21 x 21 cm (8 ½ x 8 ½ in) medium-weight iron-on (fusible) interfacing

OFFRAY RIBBONS: GROUP B

2 lengths of 25 cm x 5 mm (10 x ¼ in) feather-edged ribbon: iris

25 cm x 5 mm (10 x ¼ in) feather-edged ribbon: rust

25 cm x 13 mm (10 x ⅝ in) sheer ribbon: wine, torrid orange and hunter

2 lengths of 25 cm x 13 mm (10 x ⅝ in) sheer ribbon: purple

25 cm x 10 mm (10 x ½ in) velvet ribbon: yellow and purple

25 cm x 3 mm (10 x ⅛ in) grosgrain ribbon: yellow gold

Cotton sewing thread for tacking (basting)

Madeira metallic machine-embroidery thread no. 40: colour 490

Madeira tanne cotton no. 50: colours 580, 694 and 758

OFFRAY RIBBONS: GROUP C

11 lengths of 25 cm x 1.5 mm (10 x 1⁄16 in) double-faced satin ribbon: yellow gold

4 lengths of 25 cm x 1.5 mm (10 x 1⁄16 in) double-faced satin ribbon: grape

(For the strap — these materials will make a length of approximately 50 cm [20 in])

120 cm x 3 mm (4 yds x ⅛ in) Offray double-faced satin ribbon: bright yellow, apple green, smoke blue and grape

120 cm x 3 mm (4 yds x ⅛ in) Offray grosgrain ribbon: orchid and yellow gold

Madeira metallic machine-embroidery thread no. 40: colour 490

Madeira tanne cotton thread no. 50: orange

(For the toggle)

10 cm x 23 mm (4 x 1 in) Offray double-faced satin ribbon: yellow gold

15 cm x 3 mm (6 x ⅛ in) Offray double-faced satin ribbon: apple green and smoke blue

15 cm x 3 mm (6 x ⅛ in) Offray grosgrain ribbon: orchid

(For the loop)

2 lengths of 8 cm x 3 mm (3 x ⅛ in) ribbon (any type)

(For the lining)

EQUIPMENT

Newspaper

Old towel or piece of soft blanket

Thick household string or thick knitting yarn

2 empty matchboxes

Masking tape

2 paint 'trays' (old plates or polystyrene [styrafoam] meat trays will do), with piece of soft cloth in bottom

Broad paintbrushes

Spare pieces of fabric for practice

Iron and ironing-board

MATERIALS

23 x 23 cm (9 ¼ x 9 ¼ in) pre-washed habotai-silk (or synthetic) lining

Multi-purpose fabric paints: blue and yellow

(For making up the bags)

Ruler

Water-soluble marker pen or tailor's chalk

Machine-embroidery thread in matching colour

Sharp sewing scissors

Dressmaking pins

Dressmaker's sewing thread for tacking (basting)

Sewing needle

Iron and ironing-board

METHOD

TO MAKE THE BAG

1 Follow steps 1–12 of the method for the torn-fabric-weave bag, substituting the group A ribbons for the torn–fabric strips.

2 One at a time, and using a tapestry needle, thread the group B ribbons in and out of the basic weave. Distribute the colours as you wish, either toning or contrasting them to create different effects. Tack (baste) all the ribbons in place.

3 Thread up your sewing machine with machine-embroidery thread to tone or contrast with the ribbons within your colour scheme. Set the machine to the widest setting of zigzag stitch, and set the stitch length to create the closest stitch possible, in order to give a continual, smooth band of satin stitch (see below). Stitch a practice length on a piece of scrap fabric to check the tension.

4 Satin stitch along the length of the tacked ribbons to hold them in position and give a band of colour. Change the colours of thread as you wish (variegated threads would also create an attractive effect). Stitch along some of the wider ribbons if you feel that they need some additional decoration. Remove the tacking (basting) threads.

5 Using the tapestry needle and group C ribbons, work a running stitch through the lines of machine stitching so that the ribbons show up on the surface. You can twist the ribbons if you wish (see below).

TO MAKE THE STRAP

1 Zigzag three lengths of ribbon together with metallic thread, and stitch the remaining three lengths with the cotton thread.

2 Twist the two lengths together to form a twisted cord (see page 115).

TO MAKE THE TOGGLE AND LOOP

1 Follow the instructions given on page 123 to make the toggle.

2 For the loop, zigzag the two lengths of ribbon together with toning thread.

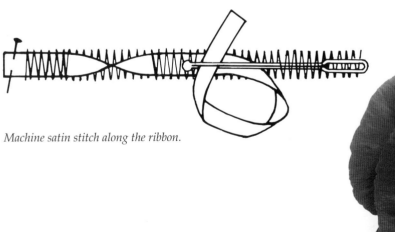

Machine satin stitch along the ribbon.

To make the printed lining

1 Cover your work area with newspaper, and lay out the old towel or piece of blanket to make a soft printing surface.

2 To make the printing blocks, wind string or thick knitting yarn tightly around each matchbox three or four times, and secure it at the top with masking tape.

3 Moisten the pieces of soft cloth in each paint tray with water. Apply fabric paint with a brush to each tray and work it well into the cloth to make a printing pad.

4 Tape a piece of practice fabric to the printing surface so that it is smooth and taut. Press a string printing block into one printing pad and apply it firmly to the fabric several times, re-charging the block with paint as necessary, and changing the direction to build up the design. Repeat with the second block and second colour to build up a 'woven' effect (see right).

5 Experiment until you feel happy with the result, and then print your lining fabric. Allow the lining to dry thoroughly, and then iron carefully to fix the fabric paint, following the manufacturer's instructions.

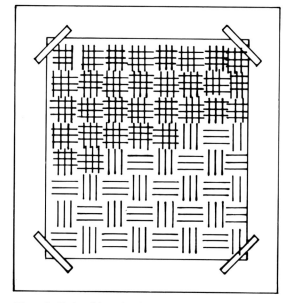

Tape the lining fabric firmly to the printing surface. Use matchbox printing blocks to build up the woven effect, creating 'layers' of colour.

Ribbon weave bag *A simple ribbon weave is decorated with machine embroidery. The twisted cord strap is machine stitched.*

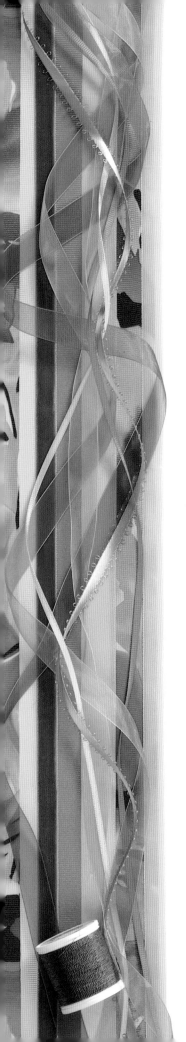

TO MAKE UP THE PANSY BAGS

1 Use the ruler and marking pen or tailor's chalk to measure out a 21 x 21 cm (8 ½ x 8 ½ in) square on the woven 'fabric'. Machine or hand stitch 5mm (¼ in) outside this square to secure the edges, then trim edges to 2 cm (¾ in) from the stitched line. Turn the fabric over.

2 Bring together two adjacent sides A and B by folding along the line XY (see diagrams opposite). Pin, tack and stitch along the marked seam line. Line up the seam directly below point X, ensuring that the distances from AB to the sides are equal. Use the point of the iron to steam the seam allowances open. If the layers of ribbon are very thick, cut them back in layered 'steps' to avoid a hard line.

3 Stitch horizontally across the base of the bag, approximately 2 cm (¾ in) up from the point on the wrong side. Carefully trim away the point using sharp scissors.

4 On the remaining two sides C and D, fold the 'fabric' to the inside along the seam line, overlapping at point CD. Pin and tack in place, stepping the layers of ribbon as before. Turn the bag the right way out, pushing out the base carefully. Press the upper edges C and D with the point of the iron.

5 Attach the strap firmly and neatly to the inside corners of the bag. Using a matching thread, attach the loop at point X, and the toggle about 6 cm (2 ½ in) from the top.

6 Mark a 21 x 21 cm (8½ x 8½ in) square on the lining fabric with marker pen or tailor's chalk. Stitch two adjacent sides right sides together, leaving a seam allowance of 1 cm (½ in). Press the seam open, and stitch across the base as for the bag. Press under the seam allowance on the two remaining sides.

7 Insert the lining in the bag. Using a matching thread, pin, tack (baste) and slip stitch the lining in place so that it is attached approximately 3 mm (⅛ in) below the ribbon edge.

8 Finally, add a tassel to the bottom of the bag (see page 117) if you wish.

Ribbons and machine thread decorate this bag which is lined with painted silk.

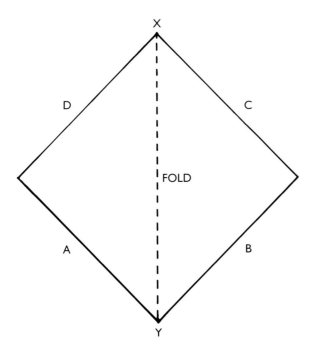

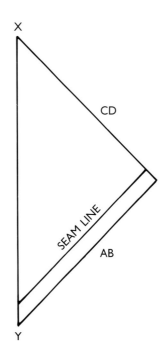

(i) Fold along line XY so that A and B come together.

(ii) Stitch along seam line AB.

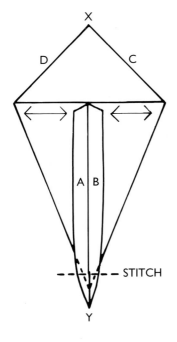

*(iii) Open out so that AB is in line with XY. Press.
Stitch across AB, approximately 2 cm (¾ in) above Y.*

BOOK COVERS

Margaret Charlton

A notebook can be turned into a unique keepsake with bright, decorative embroidery on the cover. Handmade paper for the pages, torn against a ruler to create rough edges, completes the old-fashioned feel.

BOOK COVERS

Small handmade books with luxurious embroidered covers make ideal travel notebooks, family photograph albums or personal gifts. In this project machine embroidery is worked over scraps of fabric to create a richly patterned, firm fabric with a wonderful texture. Automatic machine patterns are used, and the sumptuous effect is achieved by blending areas of colour and pattern.

Any type of sewing machine will be adequate, even if it has only a small selection of stitches such as straight, zigzag, satin, buttonhole, tricot and feather stitches – blocks of these simple stitches can be worked together effectively.

An embroidered dress from Syria provided the inspiration for the designs and colours. Automatic cross stitch, chequerboard and zigzag patterns were chosen to simulate the cross-stitch embroidery worked in different-sized squares and diamonds around the neck and down the dress front.

The most dominant colour of the embroidery was red with lesser amounts of pinks, oranges, purples and blue-greys, but brighter shades of these colours were used for the book covers to give a more vibrant, modern effect.

Find your own sources of inspiration for your book-cover designs. Magazine pictures, photographs, cards, textiles, decorated plates or flower arrangements can all provide limitless ideas for using and combining colours and patterns in original ways. Selecting the stitch patterns and colours from your source material will make your designs unique. Be bold with the colours, but avoid very dark or very light tones, as these can detract from the finished effect.

The rough texture of hand-made paper is ideal for the pages inside the book. However, this is fairly costly. Machine–made paper is an extremely good substitute. The edges are torn by a ruler for a hand–finished effect.

EQUIPMENT

Sharp sewing scissors

Iron and ironing-board

Sewing needle

Sewing machine

Paper scissors

Felt-tipped pen (in colour to match fabrics)

Pencil

Ruler

Hole punch

Tapestry needle

MATERIALS

*(MEASUREMENTS GIVEN WILL MAKE
ONE BOOK COVER)*

*60 x 60 cm (24 x 24 in) Vilene Bondaweb
(fusible webbing)*

*30 x 30 cm (12 x 12 in) felt, in one of your
chosen colours*

*Scraps of plain and/or patterned cotton,
poly/cotton, silk or any other lightweight
to co-ordinate with your chosen colour scheme*

Scraps of transparent fabric

Dressmaker's sewing thread for tacking (basting)

*Madeira cotton machine-embroidery threads
(no. 40), in a minimum of 10 colours to
co-ordinate with your chosen fabrics*

*Shiny or metallic machine-embroidery threads
(optional)*

24 x 14 cm (9 ½ x 5 ½ in) pelmet Vilene

*48 x 28 cm (19 x 11 in) cotton fabric, in a colour
suitable for the background and lining
of the book cover*

24 x 14 cm (9 ½ x 5 ½ in) sheet of scrap paper

*236 x 168 cm (94 x 67 in) sheet (A1 size) of stiff
handmade or commercial (machine-made) paper
for the book pages*

Scraps of yarn for the cord, in matching colours

*Coton à broder or silk threads for the tassels, in
matching colours*

METHOD

TO MAKE THE BOOK COVER

1 Cut a square of Vilene Bondaweb (fusible webbing) measuring 30 x 30 cm (12 x 12 in) and remove the backing paper. Place it carefully on to the felt.

2 Cut the oddments of fabric into pieces measuring approximately 3–5 cm (1–2 in) x 5–8 cm (2–3 in), varying the sizes slightly. Place the pieces on to the Bondaweb (fusible webbing), with overlapping edges, until they cover it completely (see diagram below).

3 Press with a hot iron to bond the fabrics together (see page 15).

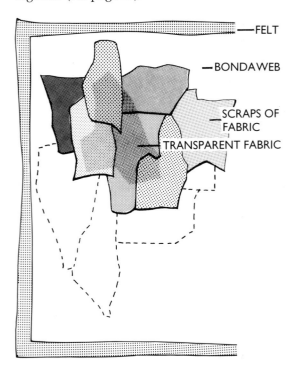

FELT

BONDAWEB

SCRAPS OF
FABRIC

TRANSPARENT FABRIC

Bonding the fabrics together

The fabrics used

4 Cut the transparent fabric into rectangles and lay these over some areas to create further colour variations. Tack (baste) them in place, and tack (baste) down any loose edges of fabric to keep them out of the way during the machining stage.

5 Thread up your sewing machine with one of the machine-embroidery threads (the order and extent to which each colour of thread is used will depend on your design). Select 3–5 automatic patterns, and experiment with these on a spare piece of fabric to see how they work together (see below). Details of how to work automatic patterns on the machine can be found on pages 31–32. A combination of solid and more open patterns often works well, as does a mixture of geometric and curved motifs.

Automatic patterns. Four of these patterns were used for each book cover.

52

Cut the fabric into pieces and place the pieces on to fusible webbing.

Machine stitch the fabric pieces using contrasting threads.

Add more stitches until the fabric is completely covered. The result is a richly textured design.

The back of the fabric is also richly textured.

6 Stitch blocks of 5–7 rows of one pattern to darn over the edges of the fabric pieces (see right). This can be done in three ways: by stitching each line separately, by using the reverse function of your machine to work backwards as well as forwards, or by turning the fabric round at the end of each row. Experiment with each method to discover which suits you best.

7 Continue working, stitching some blocks vertically and some horizontally, and using all your chosen stitch patterns and thread colours in turn, until the whole area is covered in stitchery. You can incorporate shiny or metallic threads into the final layer of stitching to provide highlights, if you wish.

8 Stitch a second layer of blocks on top to darn over the edges of the previous blocks of stitchery. Use all the patterns and colours in turn again.

9 Assess the pattern and colour balance of the work, and add further patterns and individual motifs as required. Working some of these diagonally will provide extra interest.

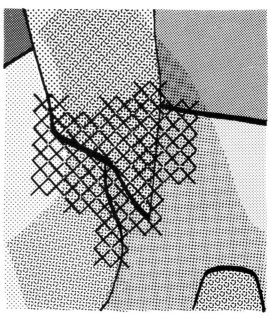

Block of pattern rows worked over the edges of the fabric pieces

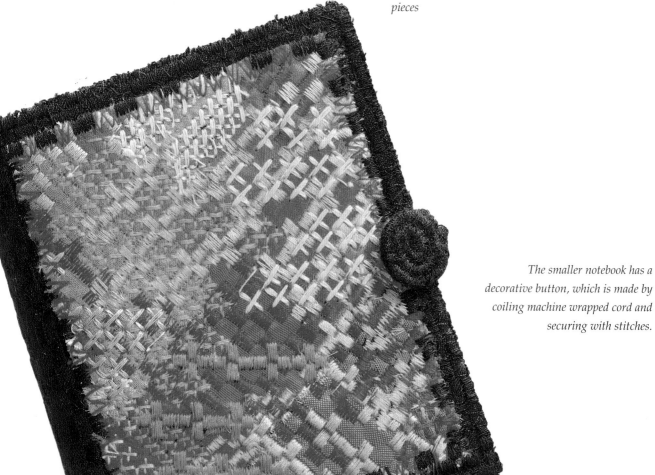

The smaller notebook has a decorative button, which is made by coiling machine wrapped cord and securing with stitches.

The front and back of the larger notebooks.
Tassels add a finishing touch.

TO MAKE UP THE BOOK

1 Cut two pieces each of Vilene Bondaweb (fusible webbing) and cotton fabric to 24 x 14 cm (9½ x 5½ in). Remove the backing paper from the Bondaweb (fusible webbing).

2 Place one piece of Bondaweb (fusible webbing) on to a piece of cotton fabric, followed by the piece of pelmet Vilene, another piece of Bondaweb (fusible webbing) and the second piece of cotton fabric. Press with a hot iron to bond the layers together. Machine stitch around the edges with zigzag stitch.

3 Cut a window measuring 13 x 9 cm (5 x 3½ in) in the piece of scrap paper, and use it as a 'frame' with which to select the two best areas of the embroidery for the front and back of the book cover. Try positioning the window diagonally as well as horizontally or vertically in order to find the most pleasing areas (you may find that a little more stitchery is needed to balance up the selected areas). Cut out the two pieces of embroidery.

4 Position each piece of embroidery in turn 5mm (¼ in) from the three edges of the book-cover ends (see below), and sew into place using machine zigzag stitch.

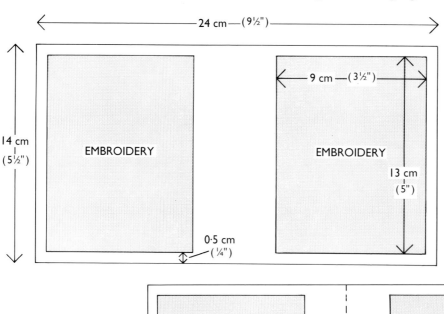

Position of embroidery on book covers

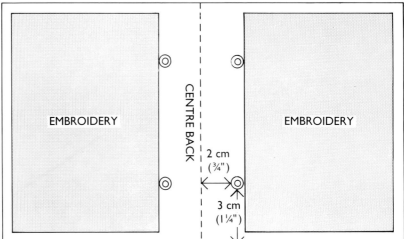

Position of eyelet holes

56

5 Work a suitable pattern in rows down the spine area of the book, and all round the edges of the book cover. If any white Vilene Bondaweb (fusible webbing) is still visible, colour it carefully with a felt-tipped pen.

6 Stitch four eyelet holes (see page 29) 3 cm (1¼ in) from the top or bottom edges and 2 cm (¾ in) from the centre back of the book cover (see diagram opposite, below).

7 Make ten double pages for the book, each measuring 21 x 13 cm (8½ x 5¼ in), by tearing the paper against a ruler to create the rough edges. Fold each piece of paper in half and punch holes to coincide with the positions of the eyelet holes.

8 Make a machine-wrapped cord (see page 116) of approximately 100 cm (40 in) in length, using machine-embroidery threads over yarns in some of your selected colours.

9 Make two tassels (see page 117) using silk or coton à broder threads, also in colours to match the embroidery.

10 Sew one tassel to one end of the cord. Insert the book pages into the cover, and then thread the other end of the cord through the cover and the inserted pages with the tapestry needle. Twist and then tie the cord ends, and attach the second tassel. As an alternative to the tassels, you can make a button-and-loop fastening from the machine-wrapped cord (see page 123). This type of fastening is suitable when thick, handmade-paper pages are used.

11 Make use of any left-over pieces of embroidered fabric by cutting them into rectangles and arranging them in a pattern to form another book cover. You can make books of any dimensions (see below), but, when designing a larger size with more pages, remember to allow sufficient fabric for the spine of the book, as this may be wider than you anticipate.

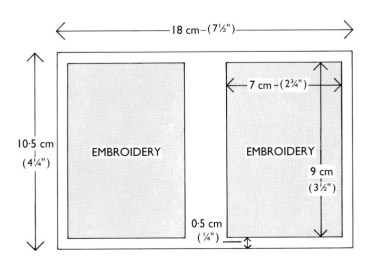

Measurements for smaller book

CUSHION WITH TASSELS

Siân Martin

The stitching on this colourful cushion is
extremely simple to work and can be
varied in almost infinite ways.
Attach tassels to the corners as shown, or
all round the cushion for a really
extravagant look.

CUSHION WITH TASSELS

This elegant hand-stitched cushion has been designed to co-ordinate with a soft-furnishing (drapery) fabric which could form part of a room decoration. Curtain fabric, a carpet, upholstery fabric or wallpaper can all be drawn on as guides for the colour scheme of your cushion and its toning tassels (for types of tassels see pages 117–121).

Take a sample of one of these materials with you, if possible, when you buy the threads and ribbons for the cushion embroidery, so that you can choose the range of colours and textures carefully. If you do not have a sample of this kind, you will need to record the colours at home before selecting from the vast range of threads and ribbons available. Use any colouring sources that you have – children's crayons, scraps of colour ripped from magazine pages, threads or fabric off-cuts – to make a colour swatch. The background fabric of the cushion is also important - select a fabric to complement and enhance your chosen colour scheme.

The embroidery consists of close rows of simple darning stitches which form rich borders around the cushion, on both the front and back surfaces. The cushion shown here has been stitched with fifteen different types of embroidery threads and five types and colours of ribbons. The central front section has been decorated with further bands of stitchery. You could work wavy parallel bands or cross-over bands to create a 'tartan' effect.

The finished cushion measures 38 x 38 cm (15 x 15 in), although the starting requirements are slightly larger than this to allow for the 'shrinkage' during the stitching process.

EQUIPMENT

Tape measure and long ruler

Sharp sewing scissors

Water-soluble fabric marker pen

Piece of scrap card of the same colour as the background fabric

Scotch tape

Range of sewing needles to suit the thickness of the chosen threads and ribbons

Masking tape

Dressmaking pins

Sewing machine

Clean paintbrush or sponge

MATERIALS

120 x 50 cm (48 x 20 in) background fabric (this need not necessarily be an even-weave fabric, as the darning stitches are worked freely). The fabric used here is a strong cotton plain-weave

Approximately 9.6 m (10½ yds) of each of 20 different-coloured and textured embroidery threads and ribbons

Dressmaker's sewing thread in a toning colour for hemming and seams

Dressmaker's sewing thread for tacking (basting)

Approximately one skein of each colour of thread used for the embroidery, for the tassels (optional)

38 x 38 cm (15 x 15 in) cushion pad (form)

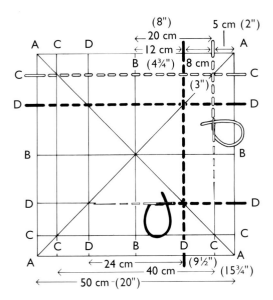

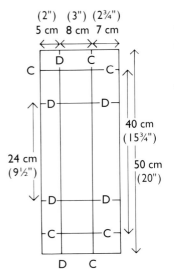

Far left *Measurements and drawn lines of the design on the cushion front and back, and the stitched outlines of the borders*

Left *Measurements and drawn lines of the design on the back flap*

METHOD

1 Cut the background fabric into two 50 x 50 cm (20 x 20 in) pieces and one 50 x 20 cm (20 x 8 in) piece, cutting straight along a line of the weave if this is visible. Tug the fabric diagonally in both directions so that each cut piece is square at the corners.

2 Using a long ruler and the water-soluble fabric marker pen, draw two diagonal lines (marked A–A see above) on both squares of fabric, and lines B–B centrally across the fabric. These lines will help you to check that

the border lines are all positioned correctly.

3 Using the fabric marker pen, draw the design on both fabric squares to show the border outlines. Make sure that the lines are parallel to the fabric edges and to each other. Lines C–C denote the outer limits of the stitched borders and the seam line. Lines D–D denote the inner limits of the borders and the central section. Draw lines C–C and D–D on the 50 x 20 cm (20 x 8 in) piece of fabric (this will form the back flap of the cushion).

Front, back and back-flap shapes for cutting from background fabric

(A) Front of cushion, showing borders and panel

(B) Main back of cushion, showing three stitched borders

and edge to form hem

(C) Back flap of cushion, showing one border and edge to form hem

(D) Back flap with one hem edge folded

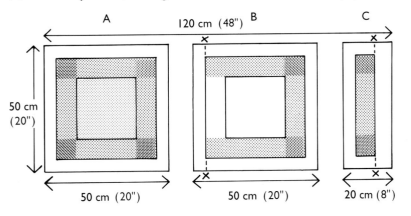

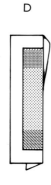

To PLAN THE COLOUR DESIGN OF THE BORDERS

1 The cushion shown has been stitched in bands of colours graded from bright to pale, on a background fabric of off-white, so that each coloured border looks as if it is gently emerging from the main background. If you have chosen a coloured background fabric for your cushion, you will need to grade your coloured threads by placing the threads which are similar in colour to the fabric together on one edge of the border; gradually build up threads of contrasting colours towards the other edge of the border.

2 To organize the threads in this way, cut a piece of scrap card, the colour of your background fabric, to a width of 8 cm (3¼ in) – i.e., the width of each border. Wrap the piece of card with Scotch tape, with the sticky side outward. Cut short lengths of each of your threads and ribbons, and place some of these on the sticky card to experiment with your preferred order of colours. Continue to add the threads and ribbons, placing them close together on the card to produce a mock 'border', so that you gain a good idea of what the finished effect will be. Stick on approximately 30–35 lengths of thread or ribbon – you can use the same thread or ribbon as many times as you like.

3 If you are not happy with the layout of colours, use the reverse of the sticky card to try a different combination. You can play around with all sorts of variations and themes, such as thick, soft threads grading to finer, shinier threads, to create interesting and unusual textures. The only 'rule' to follow is that you must place the colours most similar to the background colour on one edge of the card, grading to the more contrasting mixture of colours on the opposite edge. The completed thread card will be your main source of reference when stitching.

Below and above *The threads used for the embroidery and the tassels*

Opposite *The front and back of the cushion*

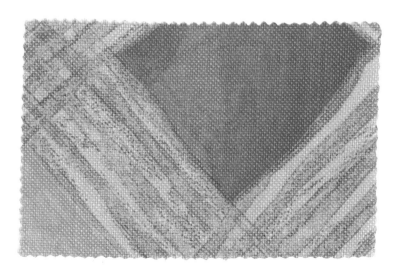

Above *The soft furnishing sample that is used as inspiration for the cushion. Reproduced by kind permission of the Designers' Guild.*

TO STITCH THE BORDERS (CUSHION FRONT)

1 Each border will be stitched right across the full length of the cushion, from seam line to seam line - i.e., from lines C–C (see diagram on page 61). To begin, select one thread or ribbon from each edge of the thread card. These will be used to stitch lines C–C and D–D. Decide which colour you would like on the outside of the border, and therefore the cushion, and which you would like on the inside of the border, or the frame of the central panel. The cushion shown here has the pale colours on the outside and the brighter colours framing the central panel.

2 You will stitch four C lines and four D lines first. These will outline the four borders so that, if the pen marks disappear, you will still be able to see your design. Begin with a stitch outside the seam line (C–C), without making a knot, leaving a length of approximately 3 cm (1¼ in) of thread on the right side of the fabric (this will be caught into the line of machining when the seam is stitched).

3 To stitch these outlines, either just make one single stitch at a time, or gather two or three stitches on the needle before pulling it through the fabric. Whichever method you use, you must allow an ease loop every three or four stitches (see below). When you have completed each row of stitching, pull the fabric (not the thread) to smooth the ease loops. If you do not do this regularly you will notice that the stitched borders will pull the fabric up so that the central panel of each cushion becomes a bulging dome!

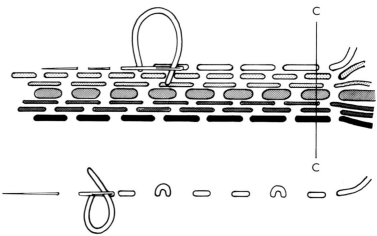

Stitched rows of different threads and ribbons, showing the stitch formation and 'ease' loop

4 Finish each row as you started it, by leaving approximately 3 cm (1¼ in) of thread on the right side of the fabric. If these loose ends get in the way when you are stitching subsequent rows, stick them down temporarily on to the fabric surface with masking tape. The placing of the stitched borders, and the way in which they overlap at the corners, can be seen in the diagram on page 61.

5 Note the length of the threads and/or ribbons that you have used to work the first eight rows of stitching, and prepare all the rest of the threads and ribbons by cutting them to the length needed for each stitched row. Be generous with thicker threads and ribbons, as they will need a greater 'ease' allowance than thin threads.

6 Stitch close rows of darning or running stitch (see below). Use a different size of stitch in each row for variety, but avoid large gaps, as this will put most of the thread on the back of the fabric so that it cannot be seen! Stitch each row within each border in the same direction – do not turn around and stitch back in the opposite direction. Each row should be stitched the full length of the border, which means that two borders will overlap in the 8 cm (3 in) square areas in the corners of the design. Work carefully as you stitch at right-angles over the existing stitches, and try not to split any stitches.

7 You may wish to stitch each border separately, or to work all four borders together by taking one thread or ribbon and stitching this on all four borders. If you wish, embellish a few rows of stitching in each border by whipping or lacing (see right).

Right Stitch variations and colour sample, showing: (A) whipped darning stitch (B) laced darning stitch

TO STITCH THE BORDERS (CUSHION BACK)

1 The main back square of fabric has three stitched borders (see diagram B, bottom of page 61). Stitch the borders exactly as you did on the front, but omitting the fourth border.

2 The back flap incorporates the fourth stitched border. Diagram C on page 61 shows that you will need to stitch two overlap areas on the ends of this back-flap border, to make the back design look the same as the front. Stitch this flap border and its overlap areas in exactly the same way as the three borders on the main back fabric, starting and finishing each row as before.

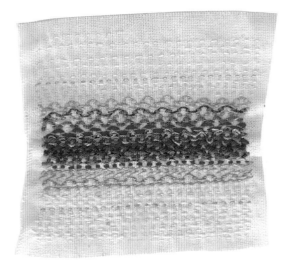

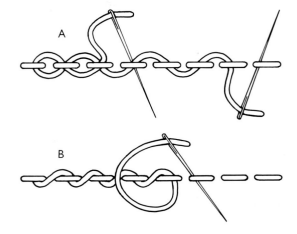

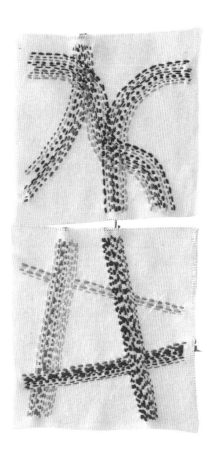

Above and on page 65: different designs for the central panel

Below: *Tassels decorate the cushion corners*

TO STITCH THE CENTRAL PANEL

1 For the panel on the front of the cushion, choose one of the three variations shown here and on page 65, or design your own variation. If you wish to change the order or number of threads and ribbons on your thread card at this stage, experiment with a different layout of colours and textures for the panel. Draw the guidelines on to the central square using the fabric marker pen.

2 The rows of stitchery in the panel will be similar to those of the borders. Stitch the rows close together, as before, using a variety of different-coloured and -textured threads and ribbons. Start and finish each row by darning the thread or ribbon through the backs of the stitches in the border areas. Whip or lace some of the rows to add extra interest if you wish.

3 If the central area of the cushion is bulging slightly because there is still too much tension in the border stitchery (in spite of the use of 'ease' loops), you will need to compensate for the bulge with the panel stitchery. Several whipped or laced rows of stitching will help, as these methods will tend to pull the fabric up a little. If you do not wish to whip or lace the stitching, use fewer ease loops in the rows of stitching. Be sure to gauge this compensation very carefully, however, as you do not want the front of the cushion to be much smaller than the back!

TO MAKE UP THE CUSHION

1 Fold, pin and tack (baste) the long edge marked 'X' of the back-flap fabric (see diagram C on page 61,) to form a hem. Machine or hand stitch firmly in place. In the same way, fold, pin and tack (baste) the edge of the main cushion back to form a hem, as indicated (see diagram B on page 61), and stitch securely.

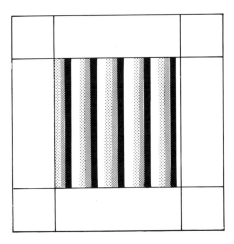

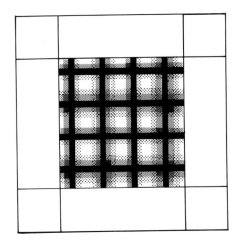

Three possible design ideas for the central panel on the front of the cushion

2 Place the back flap over the main cushion back, both with right sides facing up. Pin and then tack (baste) in position, matching the stitched borders carefully.

3 Place the back and front of the cushion with right sides together. Pin and then tack (baste) just outside the final row of stitchery. Machine stitch the seam all the way round and remove the tacking (basting) threads. Trim all the ends of the threads and ribbons, or darn them neatly into the inside seam. Trim the seam allowance to about 1–1.5 cm (½ - ⅝ in), and trim the corners diagonally.

4 Turn the cushion cover the right way out and push out the corners to make neat points. Remove any visible fabric-pen marks with a clean, damp paintbrush or sponge.

5 If you would like to add tassels to your cushion, decide on the type of tassels you would like to use (see pages 117–21), and make them up in threads used for the cushion itself. Sew the tassels firmly to the ends of the borders (see right). Finally, insert a cushion pad (form) through the back-flap opening.

Below *A back view, showing completed cushion with added tassels*

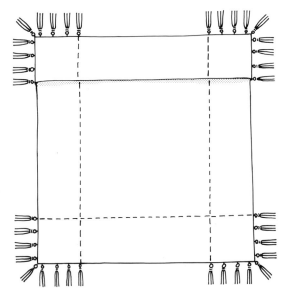

QUILTED JACKET

Ruth Issett

Colours are brushed on to the fabric to create the beautiful graded colours on this jacket. In combination with a bold geometric pattern, the finished effect is wonderfully dramatic.

QUILTED JACKET

This stunning jacket has been created from a simple pattern shape, using an unusual colouring medium (Markal PaintSticks) on black fabric. The fabric has been quilted by machine, and the stitchery surrounding the fabric-coloured areas enriches and complements the quilted effect beautifully. The simplicity of the pattern shape is ideal for a project of this kind, because it means that any design on the fabric can be used to the best effect without being spoiled by awkward seams and darts when made up.

On the jacket shown here, a simple geometric design has been used as the basic grid. Within the different sections of the grid, it has been possible to create colour variations, blending and mixing the paint sticks colours to bring about different moods. The design has been further enriched by the coloured threads used for the machine quilting. Even with a limited number of different threads, many colour combinations can be created, making the finished piece attractive and entirely original.

A background of dark-coloured or black fabric makes iridescent colours, such as those used here, even more striking, but paint sticks can be used on all coloured grounds. Before working on the fabric for your jacket, it is a good idea to experiment first with your ideas, and then to carry out an exact sample on a spare piece of the fabric that you intend to use. Try out your chosen colours to see if you are happy with the result, and work a sample of quilting, too, to gain an even more accurate idea of how the finished fabric will look.

Use your own ideas to the full in order to enhance your jacket. Explore some different colour combinations to achieve a range of effects, experimenting with coloured threads and paint sticks. The combination of stitchery and flat colour will produce unexpected results, and you may find that the most pleasing result is not, in fact, the most obvious mixture of colours.

On the jacket shown here, a variety of richly coloured threads highlight the shapes extremely effectively (see the detail on page 79).

EQUIPMENT

Pencil

Ruler

Tissue paper or other suitable paper for pattern

Paper scissors

Masking tape

Large sheet of hardboard or other smooth surface

Dressmaking pins

Tailor's chalk

Stiff brushes (old toothbrushes are ideal) – one for each colour

Iron and ironing-board

Sharp sewing scissors

Sewing machine

Sewing needle

MATERIALS

2 m x 150 cm (2½ yds x 60 in) pre-washed smooth dark-coloured or black fabric, with a simple weave (e.g., viscose panama, as used here. Markal PaintStiks will print on to any fibre, so select any fabric that you feel is suitable for the jacket). If fabric of 150 cm (60 in) width is not available, it is possible to adapt the pattern slightly by making a seam in the centre back (see Step 1 of Method)

Markal Paint Sticks in iridescent turquoise, blue, bronze, pearl, gold and purple (or other colours of your choice)

2 m x 150 cm (2½ yds x 60 in) light-weight wadding (batting), in black if available, if you are using dark-coloured or black top fabric

2 m x 150 cm (2½ yds x 60 in) dark-coloured organza (optional)

2 m x 150 cm (2½ yds x 60 in) muslin to back the quilting

Dressmaker's sewing thread for tacking (basting)

Machine-quilting threads in colours to match the fabric

2 m x 150 cm (2½ yds x 60 in) lining fabric

Matching thread to make up the jacket

METHOD

Each square equals one centimetre (one inch) on the grid overleaf.

1 Scale up the jacket pattern pieces to the size desired, on to the tissue paper or other suitable paper. Add a 2.5 cm (1 in) allowance to all seams to allow for the effects of quilting. If your chosen fabric is less than 150 cm (60 in) wide, the jacket can be made with a seam in the centre back. In this case, you will need to allow for the seam when cutting the fabric.

These paint sticks are used to decorate the fabric

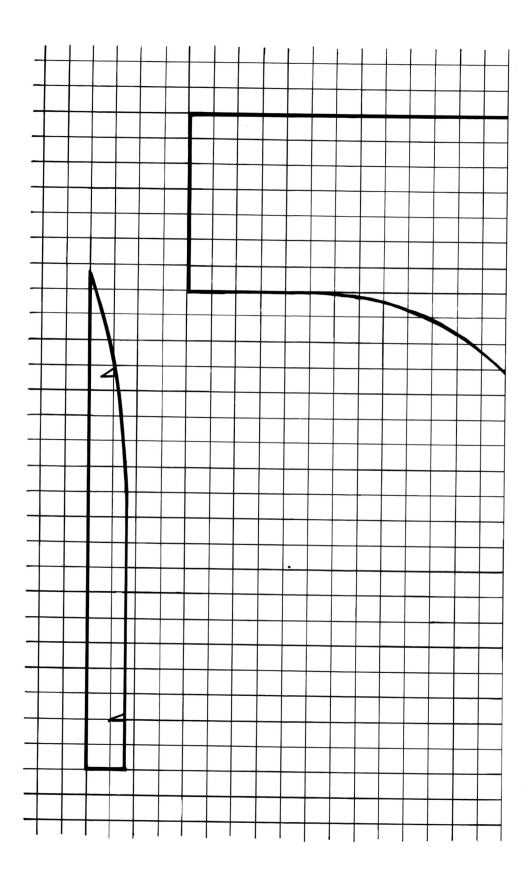

Each square = 2.5cm (1in)

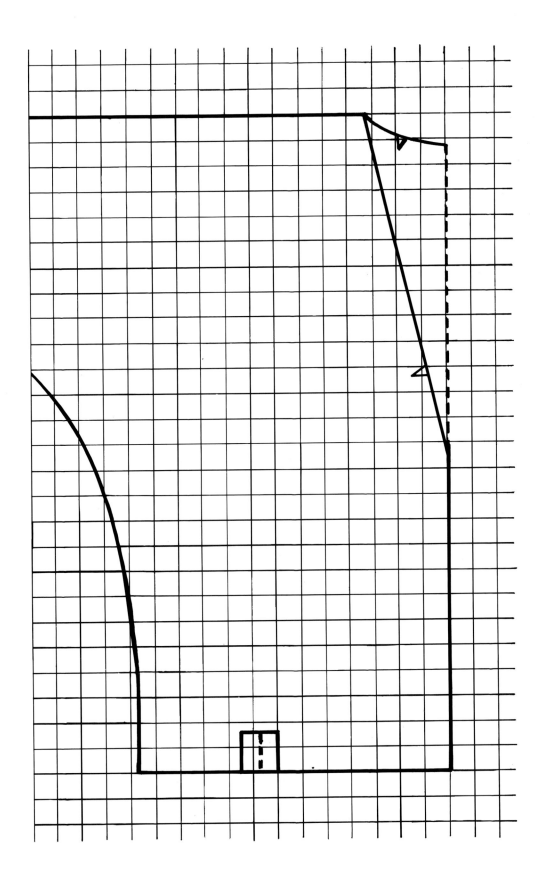

TO COLOUR THE FABRIC

1 Tape the top fabric carefully to the hardboard or other smooth surface, making sure that it is taut and attached securely on all four sides. Pin the pattern pieces on to the fabric and mark out the pieces using tailor's chalk, but do not cut them out at this stage. Using the paper pattern, work out where your design is to be placed on the fabric.

2 For this project, masking tape is used to create a range of designs based on the grid system – you can explore a range of different geometric patterns using this technique, such as lines, checks and squares. The design shown here has been worked on a 10 cm (4 in) width grid using rectangles and triangles. In places the masking tape has been lifted, re-positioned and further colour added in order to create subtle effects. When you have decided on a design, use the masking tape to mark it out on the fabric and define the areas that you wish to colour. Take care to match the pattern at the shoulder seams, at the centre front and horizontally.

3 Start to add the colour by brushing the paint stick colour off the masking tape on to the fabric (see page 25). This will create a delicate shaded effect. Begin at the centre top of the fabric and work across it, so that your hand and arm are not rubbing the areas that you have just coloured. Take care not to overload the fabric with Paint Sticks, as this

Masking tape is used to create a geometric design

will cause it to become stiff and you will lose the attractive shaded quality.

4 When you have completed the colouring, remove the tape. Leave the fabric to dry and cure for 48 hours. Iron the fabric, following the paint sticks manufacturer's instructions, to fix the design permanently into the fabric.

TO QUILT THE FABRIC

1 Lay out the coloured fabric and pin the paper pattern to it. Allowing an extra 2.5 cm (1 in) on all seams to accommodate the quilting, cut out the fabric: two fronts, one back on the fold and two collar pieces on the fold.

2 Lay the fabric right-side down on a flat surface. If your wadding (batting) is light-coloured, in contrast to the dark top fabric, it is advisable at this stage to place a fine layer of dark-coloured organza behind the top fabric, in order to prevent fibres from the wadding (batting) from pulling through during the quilting process and becoming visible on the finished jacket. Place the wadding (batting) on top, followed by the muslin, and make sure that all the fabrics making up the 'sandwich' are very flat and smooth.

3 Pin all the layers together, working from the centre out to the edges, smoothing out the fabric as you pin. Tack (baste) the layers

Colours are applied to the masking tape and an old toothbrush is used to brush the colours on to the fabric

*Iridescent colours are brushed on to black fabric, and
machine quilting is used to enhance the colours in this jacket.
A simple pattern forms the basis of the design.*

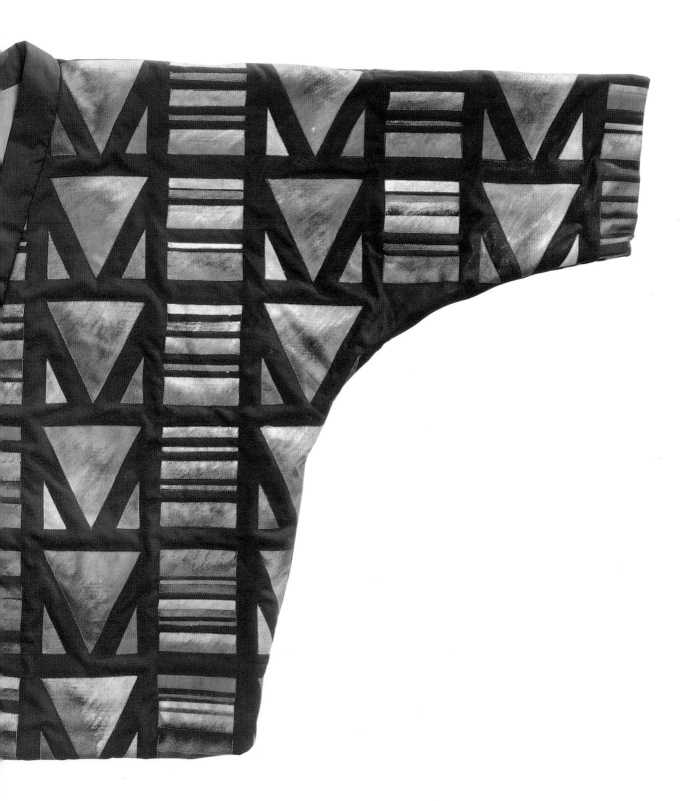

together both vertically and horizontally, again working from the centre outward, keeping the rows of stitching approximately 7.5 cm (3 in) apart. It is important to do this thoroughly, as this stitching will prevent the fabric from riding up and causing problems when you begin to quilt on the machine.

4 Prepare your sewing machine for quilting, setting it to straight stitch with a medium stitch length. Decide on the colours of machine-embroidery thread that you plan to use before embarking on the quilting, winding up bobbins as necessary. Check the stitch tension to ensure that the stitches are

The top fabric is backed by black organza and the wadding is sandwiched between the organza and muslin.

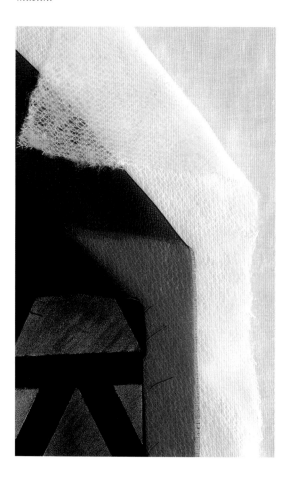

evenly spaced. Remember that the top fabric will puff up as you stitch, and that you must take care not to catch the tacking (basting) threads on the presser foot.

5 Starting once again in the centre of the fabric, select a thread which you feel is suitable for outlining an area of coloured fabric. Begin your straight stitching by making a few stitches forward and backward to secure the thread and the stitching – this will save you considerable time when finishing the jacket. Stitch around the shape, keeping as close to the edges as possible. Finish the stitching as you began it, by working a few stitches forward and backward. Carefully cut the thread close to the fabric at the front, and pull any spare thread through to the wrong side of the fabric to give a neat, firm finish.

6 Work in the first thread colour over the whole jacket, then change to the second colour and repeat the process. Continue in this way until you have used all your colours, and all the areas of fabric have been secured by stitching. Remove the rows of tacking (basting).

To make up the jacket

1 Pin each piece of quilted fabric to the corresponding pattern piece to check the size, and trim as necessary. Use the pattern pieces, still pinned to the quilted fabric, to cut out the lining fabric to exactly the same size.

2 Remove the pattern pieces. If you have used fabric of less than 150 cm (60 in) in width, pin, tack (baste) and then sew the centre back seam of the jacket with right sides together, leaving a seam allowance of

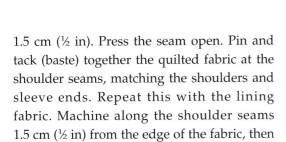

1.5 cm (½ in). Press the seam open. Pin and tack (baste) together the quilted fabric at the shoulder seams, matching the shoulders and sleeve ends. Repeat this with the lining fabric. Machine along the shoulder seams 1.5 cm (½ in) from the edge of the fabric, then press the seams open.

3 Matching the under-arm seams, pin and tack (baste) as before. Repeat with the lining fabric. Machine stitch the seams, then carefully clip the curve of the seam allowance in order to ease the fabric under the arm. Press the seams open.

4 Sew together the central seam of the collar. Press the seam open and press the fold along the fold line. Matching the centre seam of the collar with the centre of the jacket back, pin and then tack (baste) the collar into position, with the raw edges of the collar and the jacket neckline together. Stitch with a seam allowance of 1.5 cm (½ in).

5 Turn the jacket lining inside-out and place with right sides together over the jacket. Matching the seams at the shoulders and sides, pin and then tack (baste) the quilted fabric and lining together around the neckline, down the fronts and around the back. Stitch, still with the 1.5 cm (½ in) seam allowance. Do not sew the cuffs together at this stage.

6 Check that the fabric has seamed together correctly, then trim the seam allowances to give a neat finish. Trim the front bottom corners, close to the stitching at a 45° angle so that the corner will turn out to a neat right-angle.

7 Turn the jacket the right way out, pulling it through the open sleeve ends. At this point, the jacket will suddenly look almost finished, as all the untidy seams will now be concealed inside the lining. Press the lining into position. Topstitch the jacket edge with machine straight stitch, 6 mm (¼ in) from the turned edge.

8 Topstitch the tucks into the bottom edge of the back of the jacket, as marked on the pattern. This will add shape and style to the completed garment. To finish off the jacket, trim the sleeve lining so that it is slightly shorter than the outer sleeve. Turn in the cuffs and then neatly slipstitch them to the lining.

A detail of the jacket, showing how the machine quilting in toning colours enhances the geometric shapes

WALL
HANGING

Heather Marsh

*This cheerful wall hanging, with its
cheeky birds, bright flowers and foliage,
will liven up any part of the house.
It would be especially suitable for a
child's bedroom.*

WALL HANGING

Felt is one of the oldest fabrics known to man – versatile enough to be used for protection against adverse weather conditions, but also for the finest, softest carpets and even for items of clothing. Embroiderers have long recognized the beautifully smooth, tactile surface of felt as an ideal fabric for decorating with stitchery – either directly, or for softening the effect of stitching on a firmer material.

Working with felt, especially on a large scale, can be a daunting prospect for the newcomer to the technique. Even those who say they have never made felt, however, will probably admit to the classic mistake of washing a wool sweater at too high a temperature, creating exactly the conditions needed for wool to felt: i.e., water, agitation and pressure.

Preparing the fleece pile is a straightforward procedure, but making large pieces of patterned felt means that additional fleece needs to be pulled, or cut to shape and placed on the top. Although the whole parcel can be tacked (basted) together to keep the design in place, too much enthusiasm, combined with inexperience, can give unpredictable results, causing disappointment after so much work.

Bearing all this in mind, the new and really exciting method described here was developed in order to overcome such problems.

The secret is to sandwich the fleece between two layers of cold-water-soluble fabric – this will give you as many small sections as are required to make one large piece. The advantage of using this technique is that it enables many other embroidery techniques to be used as well, such as cut-work, inlay and appliqué. The seams which result from piecing the whole back together again bond in the felting process and become a further element of the overall design. The best part of all is that the whole fabric is felted in the washing-machine, eliminating the need for back-breaking work with the kitchen awash in cold soap suds!

The wall hanging shown here has been designed for a child's room, using warm, rich colours – blues, sea-greens, pinks, oranges and rust, in simple bold shapes and border patterns. The instructions given in this project can be followed exactly if you wish, but you can of course substitute any colours of your choice to complement your own design.

Right A background of felt is decorated with appliquéd silk and hand stitching

82

EQUIPMENT

Pencil

Coloured pencils or other colouring materials

Masking tape

Paper scissors

Sharp sewing scissors

Paintbrushes

Dressmaking pins

Sewing needle

Pair of hand-carders

Old sheet

Long needle

Washing-machine

Iron and ironing-board

Length of wooden dowelling and two hooks

MATERIALS

Sketching paper

Roll of old wallpaper, or other large sheets of cheap paper

4 x 1 m (4½ x 1¼ yds) light-weight habotai silk or silk lining

5 x 1 m (5½ x 1¼ yds) cold-water-soluble fabric

Silk paints in a range of colours, to include: blues, greens, warm yellow, rust and pink

Dressmaker's sewing thread for tacking (basting)

Approximately 250 g (9 oz) prepared wool fleece (see below) in each of the following colours: dark blue, mid-blue, light blue, white yellow, dark sea-green and mid-sea-green

Approximately 50 g (2 oz) prepared wool fleece (see below) in turquoise, violet and cerise

Stranded silk embroidery threads in colours to match the fleece

Strong cotton thread

50 cm x 23 mm (20 x 1 in) ribbon in a co-ordinating colour

METHOD

1 Work out your design on a reduced scale initially, using sketching paper. Bear in mind when doing this that wool can shrink by up to one-third of its original size during the felting process, and that any design details should therefore be bold. Colour in the design using your chosen colours.

2 Stick two widths of wallpaper (if using) together with masking tape, or tape together large sheets of paper to the required size. Draw out the full-sized design on the reverse of the paper. (The design shown here was drawn to 125 x 90 cm [50 x 36 in], with a centre panel of 95 x 60 cm [38 x 24 in].) This will be used as your paper pattern.

3 Cut a piece of habotai silk or silk lining, and two pieces of cold-water-soluble fabric, to the size of the centre panel plus a 25 cm (10 in) working allowance all round. Paint the silk with a mixture of blues and greens. Allow the silk paints to dry, and fix into the fabric following the manufacturer's instructions. Pin and then tack (baste) the silk to one piece of the cold-water-soluble fabric,

Opposite *A working drawing for the wall hanging, drawn to a reduced scale*

with the painted side facing inward. This will form the backing fabric for the panel.

TO MAKE THE CENTRAL PANEL

1 The first step is to card the fleece and to lay it on to the backing fabric. The purpose of carding is to make all the fibres lie in the same direction, and it is really quite easy with a little practice. First cut or pull the fleece into lengths of about 15 cm (6 in). Take one hand-carder in your left hand, with the wire face upward, and the other in your right hand, with the wire face down.

2 Beginning with the dark-blue fleece in the top right-hand corner (or your own colour in this part of the design), place two or three lengths of fibres on the left carder and then draw the right one across it gently but firmly in a single action. The movement should not be harsh, and you should finish with your hands apart. Lay down the sections of carded fleece on the backing fabric, so that they are all lying in the same direction, and overlap each other slightly.

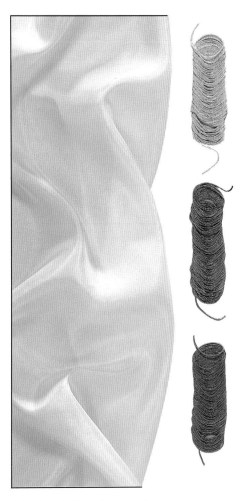

Unpainted silk and contrasting threads

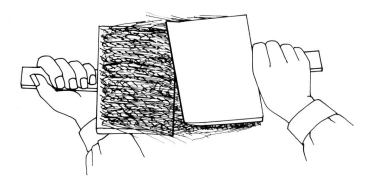

Carding the fleece

3 Continue carding and laying out the fibres in this way, gradually changing the colours of the fleece as you work across the fabric, blending into lighter blues and violet as here, or into the colours of your own design. Carry on until you have covered the whole piece of fabric with carded fibres.

4 Repeat the process, this time turning the sections so that they lie at right-angles to the first. Do this a third time to make the final layer, placing the fibres in the same direction as the first ones. Make sure that all the sections are evenly laid – thin areas could result in an uneven felt, or even holes.

Lay the carded fibres over each other in different directions

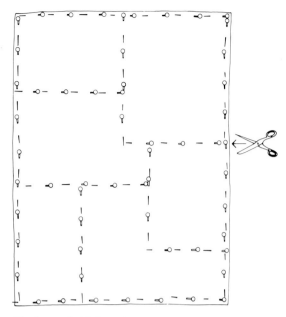

Pin the sandwich into six segments and cut them out

5 Lay the second piece of cold-water-soluble fabric on to the pile of fibres and pin it all the way round. Next, pin the sandwich into six uneven segments and, taking a deep breath, cut it into these six pieces. Using small stitches, sew round each piece to secure the fibres inside (as you will stitch all the pieces back together again later on, the placing of these seam lines is not crucial). Pin the pieces in position on an old sheet so that you do not forget their layout.

6 If you wish, work running stitch to emphasize the design, loosely following the lines and curves within it. This stitching will add to the tactile quality of the felt's surface.

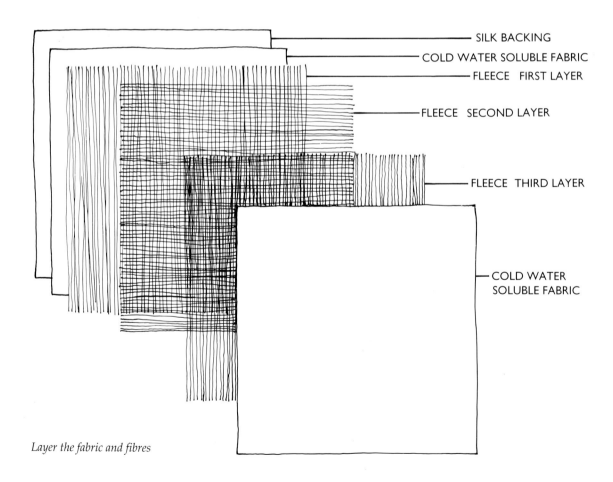

SILK BACKING

COLD WATER SOLUBLE FABRIC

FLEECE FIRST LAYER

FLEECE SECOND LAYER

FLEECE THIRD LAYER

COLD WATER
SOLUBLE FABRIC

Layer the fabric and fibres

Two strands of Madeira silk embroidery thread were used here, as the slight lustre of the thread works well with the matt texture of the wool. Use thread of roughly the same colour as the piece of fleece into which you are stitching, completing each segment in turn and pinning it back into position on the sheet. Although the running-stitch lines do not need to match the neighbouring segment exactly, try to keep the lines flowing rather than stopping abruptly at an edge.

7 Cut another piece of the habotai silk or silk lining to approximately 20 x 20 cm (8 x 8 in). Paint the silk in warm yellow, allow it to dry and fix as before, following the manufacturer's instructions. Pin the painted silk to the paper pattern, over the sun motif. Trace around the shape, slightly outside the edge.

8 Using a darker shade of yellow, work some detail in running stitch for the sun's rays. Cut out the sun, and pin and then tack (baste) it to the relevant segment (see overleaf). Stitch the motif into place (as the silk is applied directly to the fleece, and bonds with it during the felting process, there is no need to turn under the edges).

9 Add all the other motifs in the same way, applying them where you can. Stitch them to the panel along any important inner lines

Work running stitch to emphasize the design

89

(such as the wing of a bird) to add emphasis, as well as around the outer edges. Keep any motifs which should be positioned on the edge of a segment to one side.

10 Using a doubled strong cotton thread, and with wrong sides together, so that the seam sits on the surface, sew the centre panel together again. Apply the final motifs and remove all the tacking (basting) threads.

11 As the stitch tension of each embroiderer varies, the size of the panel will now differ accordingly. Measure around the panel as a guide to the required length of the first pink border. Prepare this in exactly the same way as before, by painting the silk for the backing fabric, and then building the fleece pile within the sandwich of cold-water-soluble fabric. You will probably find it easier to make a large sandwich first, pinning, tacking (basting) and then stitching it before cutting it into the correct widths; in this case, 10 cm (4 in). Join the lengths wherever necessary, as the seams will bond during the felting process. Using running stitch, and with wrong sides together, sew one width of this border all round the centre panel.

***Opposite** Details from the wall hanging*
***Below** The silk motifs are applied to the felt background using running stitch.*

90

TO COMPLETE THE HANGING

1 The two final borders are created in one piece. Make the middle border 15 cm (6 in) wide, but this time use a contrasting colour for the backing fabric. Prepare the sandwich as before, and, using torn strips of more painted silk, apply them in diamond shapes to the border, stitching on the inside and outside edges of the strips. The diamonds on this wall hanging measure 7 cm (3 in) from one opposite point to the other. When you have stitched each diamond in place, carefully cut away the top cold-water-soluble fabric and fleece – this will result in the contrasting-coloured backing silk showing through once the piece has been felted.

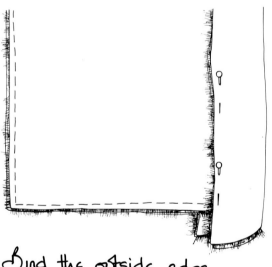

Bind the outside edge

Opposite *The back of the wall hanging, which is painted using silk paints*

2 Finish the outside edge by binding it with another fleece sandwich, 10 cm (4 in) in width (see below). This sandwich has no backing fabric. Stitch it just as you would any binding, but use strong cotton thread. The binding is decorated with more torn strips, this time applied on the diagonal.

3 To carry out the felting, take the old sheet to which the panel pieces were pinned. Place the work on one half of the sheet, and turn down the other half to make an envelope. Using a long needle, which makes it easier to stitch through all the thicknesses, and strong cotton thread, sew around the outside edges of the envelope, through the panel as well. Use very large stitches, as they will need to be taken out later (if they are too small and fine, they will felt into the panel). Work several similar rows of stitching, up, down and across the envelope, approximately 12.5 cm (5 in) apart. Be thorough with the stitching, otherwise, the 'fabric' will roll over in its envelope, and felt on to itself.

4 Place the work in a washing-machine (it needs to move freely inside, so use a commercial machine if yours is not sufficiently large). Use a wash programme with a temperature of approximately 40°C. Allow the hanging to dry naturally, then take out the holding stitches and remove the sheet. Set your iron to the wool setting, and press the felt lightly to flatten it into shape.

5 To hang the finished work, make five loops of ribbon, each 7.5 cm (3 in) long. Stitch these equidistantly to the back of the hanging, approximately 7.5 cm (3 in) from the top edge, and with the outer loops positioned 5 cm (2 in) in from the sides. Thread the piece of wooden dowelling through the loops, and screw two sturdy hooks into the wall to hold the hanging securely.

FLOWER POTS

Maggie Grey

These embroidered 'flower pots' make a
lovely decorative feature, particularly
when several of differing sizes are grouped
together. The pots are stitched by hand in
metallic and space-dyed (variegated)
threads to complement the subtle
background colours.

FLOWER POTS

The idea for making a series of pots came from a visit to a pottery exhibition. One potter had made a number of non-functional, almost flat pots and jugs, and these suggested the concept of producing textile versions of flat pots. Through subsequent experimentation, a technique evolved using pelmet Vilene, which is rigid enough to stand unsupported yet is soft enough to be stitched by hand or machine. Inspiration for the colour scheme came from a wonderful display of 'busy Lizzies' and ageratum in the garden, and the title of flower pots was born.

Instructions are given here for hand stitching two of the pots in the series. The first is decorated using satin stitch, while the second, which has a design based on the stylized shape of a cyclamen flower, uses soft gold kid (goatskin) stitched between the fabric layers to create a richly textured effect. Once you have completed one pot and have mastered the technique, try making more pots to your own designs. Look out for interesting shapes in museums and art galleries. Many objects in your home will also give you inspiration – the shapes of chair legs, light fittings and even door handles can all provide ideas. Keep the shapes simple, without too many angles, and avoid very narrow tops and bottoms.

Give your imagination full rein, too, in your choice of decoration. Automatic sewing-machine patterns can be used to create endlessly varying effects, or you could use one of your favourite cross-stitch charts to decorate a pot – try out the pattern first on a pot shape drawn on a sheet of graph paper.

The pots shown here use various stitching techniques: satin stitch and straight stitch, appliquéd gold kid (goatskin), and an automatic pattern from the memory-card facility of the New Home Sewing Machine. A Florentine counted-thread pattern is shown using pelmet Vilene which has holes punched in it making it eminently suitable for counted-thread work.

Other techniques to try could include combining padded gold kid or leather and metal threads to produce a Japanese Imari-style pot; appliqué shapes, either bonded to the Vilene or placed on top of organza, with extra stitchery; or free cross stitch. The possibilities are endless, and experi–mentation with different materials will lead on to further ideas and inspiration.

A variation on the designs for the pots shown in this chapter. Simple straight stitch forms the basis of the design.

EQUIPMENT

Photocopier

Paper

Tracing paper and pencil (optional)

Paper scissors

Dressmaking pins

Sharp sewing scissors

Bottle of Fraycheck (fabric sealant)

Small paintbrushes

Iron and ironing-board

Embroidery needle

Sewing needle

Florist's foam or wadding (batting), or strong cardboard (card), for the pot base (optional)

Large-eyed needle

MATERIALS

(FOR THE SATIN-STITCHED POT)

38 x 38 cm (15 x 15 in) pelmet Vilene

38 x 38 cm (15 x 15 in) organza

Silk paints in your chosen colours

38 x 38 cm (15 x 15 in) Vilene Bondaweb (fusible webbing)

Air-soluble fabric transfer pen or gold pen (the latter is available from stationery shops)

Space-dyed (variegated) silk thread (above)

DMC fil au clair metal thread

38 x 38 cm (15 x 15 in) each organza and Vilene Bondaweb (fusible webbing) to line the inside of the pot (optional)

Dressmaker's thread for machining, in a toning colour (above)

Strong cotton sewing thread

(FOR THE APPLIQUÉ POT)

38 x 38 cm (15 x 15 in) pelmet Vilene

38 x 38 cm (15 x 15 in) organza

Silk paints in your chosen colours

Approximately 25 x 25 cm (10 x 10 in) gold kid (goatskin) (available from needlecraft suppliers), or soft leather, painted gold

Dressmaker's sewing thread for tacking (basting)

25 cm (10 in) Madeira metallic gold cord or thick gold thread

Space-dyed variegated silk thread

38 x 38 cm (15 x 15 in) each organza and Vilene Bondaweb (fusible webbing) to line the inside of the pot (optional)

38 x 38 cm (15 x 15 in) Vilene Bondaweb (fusible webbing)

Dressmaker's thread for machining, in a toning colour

Strong cotton sewing thread

METHOD

TO MAKE THE SATIN-STITCHED POT

1 Photocopy the pattern, enlarge the photocopy to twice the size (see pages 23–4) and cut out the pattern (see right). Pin the pattern on to the pelmet Vilene and cut out two pot shapes. Cut out two more pot shapes from the organza, and seal the edges of the fabric with Fraycheck (fabric sealant), following the manufacturer's instructions.

2 Using the silk paints as directed on pages 26-7, paint both the pelmet Vilene and the organza. Allow the paints to dry thoroughly, undisturbed, and then fix according to the manufacturer's instructions.

3 Cut out the basic shapes in Vilene Bondaweb (fusible webbing), peel off the backing paper on both sides; and place between the pelmet Vilene and organza shapes. Press with a hot iron to bond the

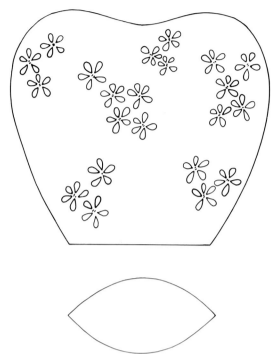

Satin stitch flower design
Enlarge this to twice the size and use it as your pattern.

fabrics together (see page 14–5). Do not worry if the resulting 'sandwich' wrinkles at this point. This will add to the finished effect.

4 Draw the flower shapes on to the organza using an air-soluble fabric transfer pen or a gold pen – the gold pen gives an attractive effect if some areas are allowed to remain visible. Suggested placements are shown in the diagram above, but feel free to re-arrange the flowers and straight-stitch motifs in order to make up your own design. Groups of odd numbers of flowers (threes or fives) give a better result than even numbers. Do not add the small triangle shapes at this stage.

Satin stitch and straight stitch decorate this pot.

5 Beginning with a knot on the wrong side of the fabric, work the satin-stitch flowers in space-dyed (variegated) thread, angling the stitches as shown below. Finish by making several stitches on the reverse of the fabric in the same place as the starting knot. If the thread twists while you are stitching, allow it to hang loose from the fabric so that it can unwind. Work one or two small straight stitches for each of the flower centres.

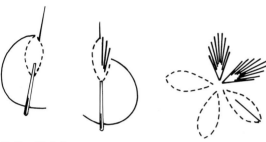

Satin-stitch flowers

6 When you have completed all the flower shapes, add the small straight-stitch triangles (see below). Work these freely in the spaces between the flowers.

7 Neaten the wrong side of the stitching by snipping off any loose threads, being careful not to cut any stitches. If the stitching looks untidy, cut two more pieces each of organza and Vilene Bondaweb (fusible webbing) to size. Peel off the backing paper from the Bondaweb (fusible webbing), place it over the back of the stitching with the organza on top, and fuse with a hot iron (see pages 14 – 15).

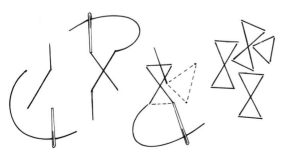

Straight-stitch triangles

8 Join the two sides of the pot by placing them with the wrong sides together and machine stitching with a toning thread, leaving a 3 mm (⅛ in) seam allowance.

9 To make a base, which will be needed if you wish to use the pot as a container for pot-pourri or as a 'keepsake' pot, hold the slightly opened pot over a piece of pelmet Vilene and draw the shape of the bottom of the pot. Cut out the shape. Fit and pin the base piece into the bottom of the pot so that the edges are level (see below). Using small running stitches, sew the base firmly to the sides of the pot. (If you stitch along the centres of the sides first, you will find it easier to sew the angles in the corners.)

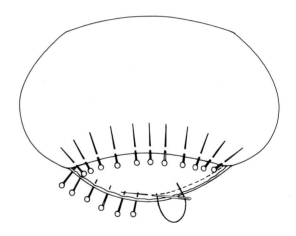

Sew the base to the sides of the pot

10 Alternatively, if no base is required but you wish to give the pot a firm shape, one option is to fill it with florist's foam or wadding (batting), which will allow the pot to stand well by itself. Another method is to shape the pot by making a cardboard (card) spacer. To do this, take a piece of strong cardboard (card) (see diagram overleaf). Measure the width of the pot about halfway up the side, and cut a strip of cardboard to

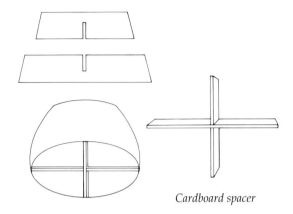

Cardboard spacer

this length and 2 cm (¾ in) wide. Angle the ends of the strip to meet the contour of the pot.

11 Hold the pot so that it fills out to the required fatness and measure that width, again about halfway up the side. Cut another strip of cardboard (card) to this length and 2 cm (¾ in) wide, and angle the ends as before. Cut away a groove in the centre of each strip of cardboard and check that they fit together snugly (see above). Take care to ensure that the grooves are correct for the angles at the ends of the strips. Fit the longer strip in its required position, then insert the shorter strip so that the grooves meet and push home inside the pot. Make any minor adjustments to the strips as necessary.

TO MAKE THE APPLIQUÉ POT

1 Decide on the required shape of the pot (or use the pattern for the satin-stitched pot). To make a pattern, draw one half of the pot shape on paper, fold it in half and cut through both halves to produce a template. Make this slightly wider than the desired width of the finished pot to allow for the curvature. If you are unsure about using a particular shape, cut it out in pelmet Vilene and then tack (baste) it together – this will give you a good idea of whether the shape will work before you spend time on the stitching. Pin the pattern on to the pelmet Vilene and cut out two pot shapes. Cut out two more pot shapes from organza, and seal the edges of the fabric with Fraycheck (fabric sealant), following the manufacturer's instructions.

Secure the gold kid (goatskin) with a few large stitches.

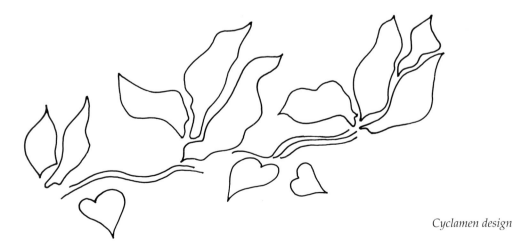

Cyclamen design

2 Using silk paints as directed on pages 26 – 27, paint both the pelmet Vilene and the organza. Allow the paints to dry thoroughly, undisturbed, and then fix according to the manufacturer's instructions.

3 Make a tracing or photocopy of the cyclamen design (see opposite, below) and cut out the main shapes from the gold kid (goatskin) or painted leather. Place these on the pelmet Vilene, either following the design shown here, or making up your own layout by moving the flowers about until you are pleased with the arrangement. Secure the leather pieces by making a few large stitches right across each petal to hold them in place.

4 Thread the gold cord or thick gold thread into a large-eyed needle and push it through from the back to the front of the pelmet Vilene, leaving 1 cm (½ in) of cord or thread at the back. Tack (baste) the cord or thread in place with metallic gold thread, using just a few stitches here and there, and at the bottom of the stem take the end through to the back of the work. Cut off the cord or thread, leaving 1 cm (½ in) for fastening off. Stitch both ends of the cord or thread to the back of the pelmet Vilene with small, neat stitches.

5 Place the organza over the pelmet Vilene, and pin and then tack (baste) it into place around the edges of the pot.

6 Using space-dyed (variegated) thread, stitch around each leather petal and leaf with small, neat back stitches. This will make the leather look as if it has been quilted. Work extra rows of stitching around the leaves. Work further back stitches along the stems, but leave gaps in places, as too much stitching at the top and bottom may make the stems look too heavy. Remove the holding stitches.

7 When you have completed all the stitching, neaten the wrong side by snipping off any loose threads. Carefully remove the tacking (basting) stitches. If the stitching looks untidy, you can, if you wish, cut two more pieces each of organza and Vilene Bondaweb (fusible webbing) to size. Peel off the backing paper on both sides of the Vilene Bondaweb (fusible webbing), place it over the back of the stitching with the organza on top, and fuse with a hot iron (see pages 14 – 15).

8 For the front of the pot, cut strips of Vilene Bondaweb (fusible webbing), peel off the paper and place the strips as close to the stitching as possible. Press carefully with the point of a hot iron to fuse. Work outward from the stitching, cutting strips and pressing with the point of the iron until the front is complete.

9 Follow Steps 8–11 of the instructions for the satin-stitched pot to complete the pot.

CRYSTAL CUSHION

Julie Smith

Fabric transfer crayons are used to develop the design for this cushion on paper, which is then transferred to fabric through a stencil. The edges of the embroidery are quilted with gold thread to create a beautifully textured surface.

CRYSTAL CUSHION

The colourful embroidery on this cushion has been worked in twisted chain stitch on a plain-coloured soft-furnishing fabric. The stitched design was based on a pattern of sweeping arcs drawn on paper with transfer crayons, which was then transferred, through a stencil, on to the fabric to form the colour guide for the stitching.

Fabric transfer crayons are ideal for use as a design basis for stitchery, and come in a range of basic colours which may be blended on paper to give subtler tints and tones before being transferred to fabric. The shades used for this cushion were inspired by a painting by the French painter Henri Lebasque, entitled *Promenade en Barque*, and the rich yellow, blues, greens and pinks stand out beautifully on the neutral background fabric. The shapes are quilted with an outline of gold thread, to 'puff up' the embroidery a little and also to promote the texture of the threads.

The design shown here is based on a repeated motif of a row of three triangles and an 'accent' shape. The pattern was repeated eight times on the front of the cushion, and its negative repeated eight times on the reverse. You could of course make another arrangement or use a completely different motif, but it is a good idea, particularly at first, to use shapes with straight edges, as these are easy to cut out accurately for use as a template. Repeating a small motif to make a design is very simple, and means that, once you have the basic motif, most of the design work has already been done. You can then duplicate the design, or parts of the design, as many times as you wish, in whatever layouts you choose. The diagram opposite shows just three of the many design possibilities which could be created with this simple motif.

The materials requirements listed here will make a cushion with a finished size of approximately 35 x 30 cm (14 x 12 in), but you can make your cushion larger or smaller as you wish, by increasing or decreasing the materials as necessary.

EQUIPMENT

Fabric transfer crayons (opposite)

Masking tape

Pencil

Metal ruler

Craft knife

Dressmaking pins

Iron and ironing-board

Embroidery needle

Sharp sewing scissors

Clean soft towel or padded surface

Quilting needle

MATERIALS

2 sheets of 60 x 45 cm (24 x 18 in) stiff white paper

30 x 21 cm (12 x 8½ in), or A4, sheet of white card (cardboard)

1.2 m x 90 cm (48 x 36 in) plain-coloured soft-furnishing (drapery) or similar fabric

2 skeins each of DMC cotton perle threads (overleaf) in a range of blues, greens, yellow and pinks (colours used here: blues 995, 517, 791, 809; greens 734, 470, 834; yellow 743; pinks 754, 758, 402, 517)

Gold thread for outlining/quilting stitched shapes (optional)

75 x 37.5 cm (30 x 15 in) medium-weight wadding (batting) for quilting (optional)

75 x 37.5 cm (30 x 15 in) muslin to back the quilting (optional)

Dressmaker's sewing thread

Approximately 3 metres (3¾ yds) piping

35 x 30 cm (14 x 12 in) cushion pad (form)

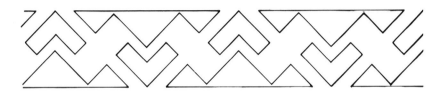

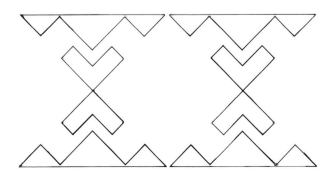

Possible layout variations using the basic motif of three triangles and an 'accent' shape

Method

To colour the fabric

1 Tape one of the sheets of stiff white paper securely to a flat surface, so that it does not move as you work. Break the transfer crayons approximately into thirds or halves and, using the sides, make sweeping semi-circular movements over the paper. The arcs should be fairly large, and should cross over each other in differing directions to create a blend of colours. Blend as many colours as you need to match your source of inspiration as closely as possible, remembering that this will be a guide to help you to place your coloured threads, but that you can change your mind later if you wish! When you have covered the paper with a layer of colour, place it to one side.

2 The next stage is to cut the template. Draw your chosen motif(s) on to the piece of white card (cardboard) and cut it (them) out, using a ruler and craft knife. With the template as a guide, draw the motif(s) on to the second sheet of stiff white paper, either following the design of this cushion or in the arrangement of your choice. Using the ruler and craft knife, carefully cut through the pencilled lines to create the stencil through which you will iron your transfer colours.

3 Place the template over the sheet of crayonned paper and carefully move it around until you like what you see through the 'windows'. Pin the two sheets of paper together around the edge, place the ruler against the edge of the design and trim the outer edge, thus giving yourself a ruler's-width border around the coloured area.

4 Cut the piece of soft-furnishing (drapery) or other fabric in half. Put one piece aside, and cut the second piece in half again to make two pieces measuring 60 x 45 cm (24 x 18 in). Lay out one fabric piece on a flat surface, then place the pinned papers on top of the fabric, coloured-side down. Pin the 'sandwich' together. With the iron on a medium setting, iron over the paper, following the crayon manufacturer's instructions. Without moving the papers, carefully lift one corner to see whether the colour has transferred. If not, replace the paper and continue ironing until it does. When all the design has transferred, lift the two papers and remove the pins.

Opposite *The crayon design and stencil*

5 The stencil will now have on it the opposite, or 'negative', image to the one on the fabric. Place the second piece of fabric on the work surface and pin the stencil on to it, coloured-side down. Iron the paper as before to transfer the design to the fabric.

6 Take the remaining uncoloured piece of fabric, cut it in half, and repeat the colouring process on one half only. Set the coloured and uncoloured pieces of fabric aside (these will be used to make the decorative edging for the cushion).

To stitch the design

1 The stitching used for this cushion is a twisted chain stitch (see below), which creates an attractive textured effect, but you could use another type of stitch, or stitches, to give a different appearance. Working with one colour of thread at a time, stitch the design on each piece of fabric in turn, following the coloured pattern. On this cushion, stitches have been stitched over other stitches where the design had colour over colour in differing directions, which also adds to the finished texture.

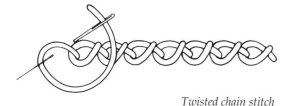

Twisted chain stitch

2 When you feel that the stitching is complete, refer back to your paper pattern and decide whether you have included all the surface stitchery you require (it is easy to 'lose' areas of overlaying stitchery when transferring the paper design, as what was on the top appears on the bottom on the fabric!) When you are satisfied, place the fabric face-down on a clean, soft towel or other padded surface and gently press the work.

3 If you wish, you can now quilt the fabric pieces. When the coloured shapes are outlined with quilting, this makes them 'puff up' a little and enhances the surface texture very attractively. To do this, cut the pieces of wadding (batting) and muslin in half. Lay the fabric face-down on the work surface, and place the wadding (batting) and then the muslin on top. Pin the 'sandwich' together, then tack (baste) across it both vertically and horizontally in rows approximately 2.5 cm (1 in) apart, in order to hold the layers firmly in place. Thread up the quilting needle with gold thread, and work the quilting around the edges of the shapes to outline them. When all the quilting is complete, carefully remove the tacking (basting) threads. Repeat with the second piece of fabric. If you do not wish to quilt the fabric, outlining the coloured stitching in gold thread can still be used to create an attractive effect.

4 Trim both pieces of fabric so that they are approximately 2.5 cm (1 in) larger than the intended finished size of the cushion, and round off the corners. This will give a nicer finished shape, and will also make it easier to attached the folded points for the edging.

TO MAKE THE DECORATIVE EDGING

1 The decorative triangles on the cushion shown here have been stitched so that they overlap each other, but you can add more or less triangles as you wish, and space them evenly or unevenly. Take the unused coloured and uncoloured pieces of fabric, and cut several long strips, approximately 5 cm (2 in) wide, from each, along the grain of the fabric. Following the diagrams below, fold down a narrow edge of fabric along the length of each strip, and press lightly to hold in place. Fold down a corner of fabric, as shown, and press, then fold down the opposite corner and press. Cut off the remaining strip and you will have one folded triangle. Repeat this process to make as many triangles as you wish.

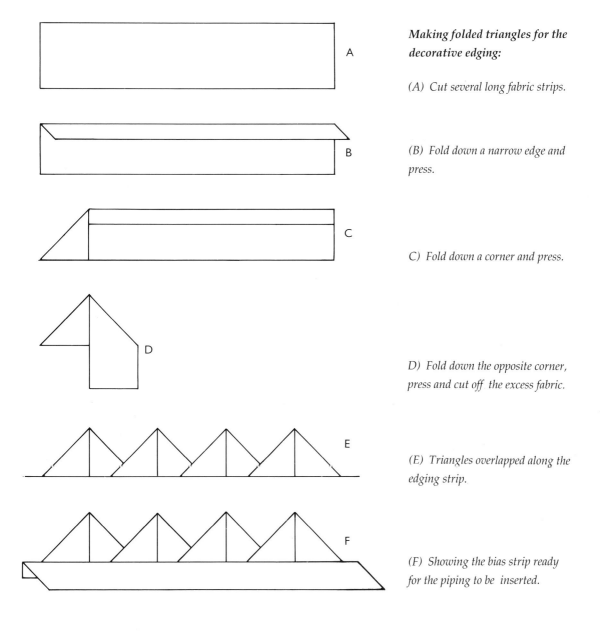

Making folded triangles for the decorative edging:

(A) Cut several long fabric strips.

(B) Fold down a narrow edge and press.

C) Fold down a corner and press.

D) Fold down the opposite corner, press and cut off the excess fabric.

(E) Triangles overlapped along the edging strip.

(F) Showing the bias strip ready for the piping to be inserted.

2 A piped edging used in conjunction with the folded triangles gives a very professional finish, and, as either side of this cushion can be displayed, a double row of piping is used, on either side of the folded triangles. To make the piped edging, cut long strips approximately 5 cm (2 in) wide from the coloured or uncoloured remaining pieces of fabric on the bias, machining them together as necessary to make two single strips, each slightly longer than the four cushion edges.

3 Fold the strip in half lengthways, with wrong sides together, and pin and then tack (baste) the triangles in place along the length, with the rough edges together. Position some triangles facing up and others down, and alternate plain and coloured triangles as you wish. To insert the piping, follow the diagrams below. Place half the piping in the centre of one strip, fold the strip over the piping and pin. Machine stitch through the strip, close to the edge of the piping. Repeat

with the second strip and then pin this over the first strip, so that the triangles are in the middle and facing inward. If you do not wish to use piping, simply fold the strips for the edging in half lengthways and press.

4 To join the edging to the main cushion pieces, place the front and back cushion pieces with right sides together. Pin the piped edging between the cushion pieces, with the piped (or folded) edges inside, the triangles pointing inward and all rough edges aligned and facing outward (see diagram). Ease the edging around the corners to fit. Machine stitch around three edges of the cushion, but stitch the edging to one side only on the fourth edge so that the cushion pad can be inserted. Trim the seam.

5 Turn the cushion cover the right way out and then insert the cushion pad through the unstitched opening. Oversew the fourth edge neatly by hand to close.

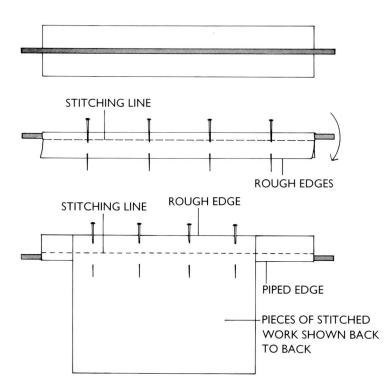

STITCHING LINE

ROUGH EDGES

STITCHING LINE   ROUGH EDGE

PIPED EDGE

PIECES OF STITCHED WORK SHOWN BACK TO BACK

How to insert the piping:

(A) Place the piping in the centre of one strip.

(B) Fold the strip over the piping, pin and machine stitch close to the piping.

(C) Pin the piped edging between the cushion and machine stitch.

Front and back of the cushion

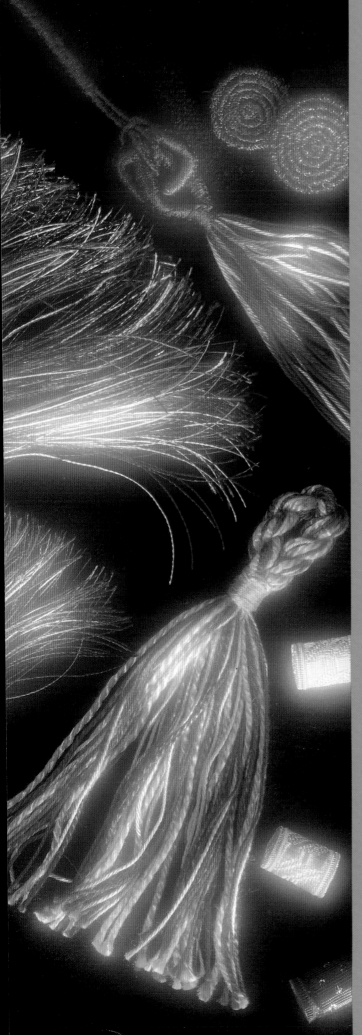

CORDS,
TASSELS
&
BUTTONS

Pamela Watts

The addition of silky tassels or fringing, intricately woven cords or bright buttons and toggles will provide the perfect finishing touch for all kinds of embroidered clothes, soft furnishings and accessories. The only limit to what you can do is your imagination!

CORDS TASSELS & BUTTONS

The projects shown in this book include a range of finishings, instructions for which are given here. A special finishing technique adds interest and individuality to any embroidered item, and, once you have tried the basic method, it is always worthwhile taking a little extra time to try out some of the suggested variations, as well as others which will occur to you. You may find that altering the given sizes, colour schemes or choice of threads suits a particular purpose better, for instance, or you could per-haps adapt your favourite finishing technique for use on a project other than the one specified.

Whatever you decide, the cords, tassels and other decorative touches described here will provide you with a store of ideas for these projects and for any other embroidered items that you may make in the future.

HAND-BRAIDED CORDS

The familiar three-strand braid is normally worked with three lengths of the same type of thread; yet it would look completely different if you were to use, for example, one length of ribbon, one thin thread and massed fine threads for the third strand.

Textured or metallic threads, and ribbons, can also be combined to create eye-catching effects, and the different thicknesses can produce either a delicate, thin braid or a much stronger, thicker one. Try braiding braids together. The permutations on this simple technique are endless, and the completed braids can be used for bag handles, as edgings for cushions or as surface decoration.

1 Cut three bundles of threads to one-and-a-half times the required length of the finished braid. Pin one end of each bundle into a cork or polystyrene (styrofoam) board.

2 Braid down the whole length of the threads, and finish by wrapping both ends of the braid securely with thread.

Making a hand-braided cord

114

TWISTED CORDS

Twisted cords can be made to any thickness and from a mixture of thick and thin threads and ribbons.

1 Select a variety of threads and/or fine ribbons, and measure off three times the required length of the finished cord.

2 Knot a loop at each end, and place one of these loops over a fixed hook. Insert a pencil into the loop at the other end, and move away from the fixed end so that the threads are taut.

3 Twist the pencil round and round until the cord looks tight and begins to curl. Hold the central point, and double the cord back on itself with the two ends together. Let it hang, and it will twist automatically into a tightly coiled cord. Wrap the ends with thread to secure.

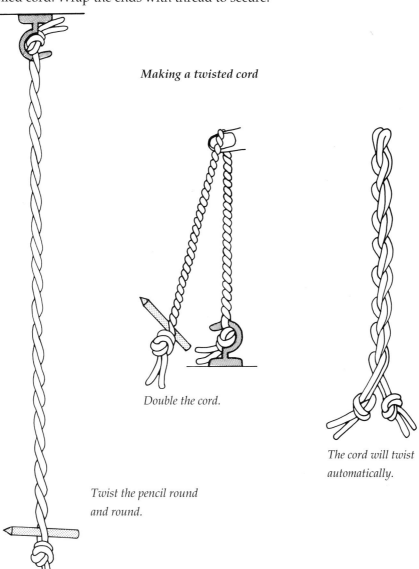

Making a twisted cord

Double the cord.

The cord will twist automatically.

Twist the pencil round and round.

MACHINE-WRAPPED CORDS

Machine-wrapped cords have similar purposes to handmade cords. They are very attractive when used on their own, but look even better if they are braided or twisted. Try adding a machine-wrapped cord to ribbons or other threads to make a twist or a braid.

METHOD A

A simple method of making a machine-wrapped cord is to use a braiding foot, which is normally used to couch down threads and thin ribbons. Most sewing machines will take this special foot, although it may not be included with the standard feet supplied. Ask your supplier whether a braiding foot is available to fit your machine.

Once you become confident with the technique, experiment with the stitch-length setting to achieve different effects. A close or satin-stitch setting will cover the yarn completely with the machine thread, whereas a longer stitch length will allow the colours of the yarns used to show through.

1 Choose a thick yarn or a mixture of finer threads, crewel yarns and cotton perle, checking that they will pass through the round hole in the braiding foot. Thread up the machine with your chosen colour of machine-embroidery thread, and set it for zigzag with the maximum stitch width.

2 Thread the yarn through the hole in the braiding foot, holding it and the two machine threads at the back of the machine.

3 With your other hand, hold the yarn firmly at the front of the machine so that, as you begin stitching, the yarn is covered with the machine stitching. Take care to ease the yarn

through evenly as you stitch. The rate at which you do this will determine how closely covered the cord will be – a little practice will soon give you the result you require.

METHOD B

If you do not have a braiding foot, it is possible to make machine-wrapped cords using either a darning foot or no foot at all.

1 Lower the feed dog (teeth) and set the stitch length to the closest satin stitch possible. Thread up the machine with machine-embroidery thread and set it for zigzag. Remember to lower the presser-foot lever in order to engage the top tension.

2 Hold the yarn or threads as described for Method A, easing them evenly through the machine as you stitch.

Machine-wrapped cords, showing closer and wider zigzag stitch worked over the yarn

MAKING A TASSEL

A basic tassel has any number of uses in decorative embroidery, and is deceptively simple and quick to make. Choose threads in colours to match those of the embroidered item, or alternatively, select bright, contrasting shades for visual impact.

1 Cut a piece of card to the required length of the tassel. Select four or five threads of different colours and types, which have been used in the main embroidery.

2 Holding the ends together, wrap the threads around the card two or three times, before cutting them along one edge.

3 Take a short length of strong thread and put both ends through the eye of a needle. Keeping the bundle of threads folded in half, slip the needle under the threads at the middle and back through the loop, pulling tight. Make an extra stitch through the loop to make it really secure.

4 With a matching or contrasting thread, wrap round and round the bundle of threads a little way down from the top, to form the neck of the tassel. Tie off the threads and then pass them through the neck into the skirt of the tassel to conceal them. Put the two threads from the top of the tassel into a needle and either sew them into a seam or on to the edge of the embroidered item.

LOOPED TASSELS

As a variation on the basic tassel described above, try putting a few thin threads into a large-eyed needle and stitching directly into the seam edge of the embroidered item to make a looped tassel.

1 Make a hole with a stiletto (awl), as near to the edge of the item as possible. Take the needle into this hole two or three times, keeping the loops of thread even, before moving along inside the seam to the position of the next tassel. Repeat the process.

2 Wrap the neck of each tassel with a matching or contrasting thread, taking this through the head, into the seam edge and along to the position of the next tassel.

Making a basic tassel

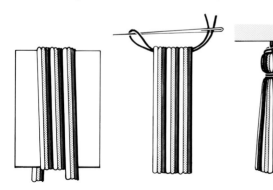

Making a looped tassel

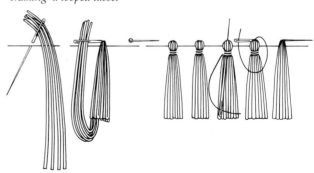

TASSELS ON AN ARMENIAN EDGING STITCH

Armenian edging stitch is very simple to work. It makes a decorative edging on its own, but also provides another means of attaching tassels to an embroidered item. Vary the colours in each tassel, group them together or space them evenly or unevenly.

1 Work the edging stitch using a firm thread such as cotton perle. Select the threads for the tassels, wrapping them around a piece of card as described on page 117, and then cut along one edge of the card.

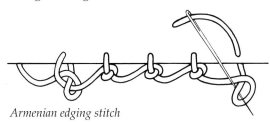

Armenian edging stitch

2 Take five or six threads, depending on the thickness of the threads and required size of the tassel, and thread them into a tapestry needle. Pass through one of the loops of the edging stitch, and level the threads at the bottom. Remove the needle.

3 Wrap the neck of the tassel and tie off the threads as described on page 117.

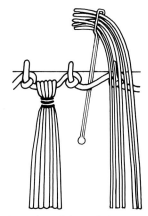

Adding to Armenian edging stitch

BRAIDED-HEAD TASSEL

This is a unique tassel that would look attractive on an item which also uses braided cords. It is easy to attach, as a cord can be slipped through the loop head and attached to the surface or edge of the embroidery.

1 Fix two long or glass-headed pins securely into a cork or polystyrene (styrofoam) board, spacing them twice as far apart as the required finished length of the tassel.

2 Take the ends of a number of reels of thread, and knot them together over one of the pins. Wrap round and round between the

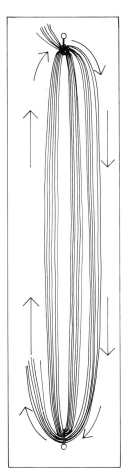

Making a braided-head tassel

two pins until the bundle of threads is half the required thickness of the tassel.

3 Carefully remove one of the pins, and cut the loops of thread. Divide into three roughly equal parts and then braid together. Secure the end of the braid temporarily with a piece of Scotch tape or a bulldog clip in order to prevent it from unravelling.

4 Mark the centre point of the length of braid. Measure a distance of 2.5–5 cm (1–2 in) on both sides of the centre point, and wrap securely with thread.

5 Release the braid from the board, folding the head into a loop so that the two wrapped points are side by side. Wrap these together to form the neck of the tassel. Unravel the two sides of the braid below this point.

TWISTED-HEAD TASSEL

This tassel would make an ideal complement to a project which uses twisted cords. It can be attached to an embroidered item in the same way as the braided-head tassel.

1 Make a length of twisted cord as described on page 115, twice the length of the required tassel. Fold the cord in half and form a loop for the head of the tassel.

2 Wrap the neck securely with thread before unravelling both ends of the cord to make the skirt. To make a fatter tassel, combine two or more lengths of twisted cord, wrapping and unravelling in the same way.

Fold the braided head into a loop and secure.

Multi-coloured threads are used to make this braided head tassel.

at these points. Set your machine for zigzag with the maximum stitch width, and use either a darning foot or no foot.

3 Zigzag over the central portion between the two tied points, using a close satin stitch. It may help to twist the bundle of threads loosely as you stitch, in order to keep them within the sideways swing of the needle. Remove from the machine.

4 Experiment with knotting the zigzagged portion into a pleasingly shaped head before wrapping the two sides together to form the neck and skirt of the tassel.

Knotted-head tassels

KNOTTED-HEAD TASSEL

The technique for machine-wrapping a cord (see page 116) can easily be adapted to make a knotted-head tassel. It can be made to any size by altering the length of the wrapped, knotted part and the skirt.

1 Take a bundle of fine machine-embroidery threads, 18–20 cm (7–8 in) long and half the required thickness of the tassel (remember that the thickness of the bundle should not exceed the width of the hole in the base plate of your sewing machine).

2 Mark off a distance of 2.5-5 cm (1-2 in) from either end, and tie the bundle together

Making a machine-wrapped cord

These beautifully coloured tassels will add a perfect finishing touch to your embroidered project

FRINGING

Instead of making individual tassels to decorate the edge of a cushion or bag, you could add a looped-on fringe using the Armenian edging stitch described on page 118. This is a very quick and easy technique, and, again, gives great scope for different spacings and colour arrangements. With some fabrics, it is possible to pull out threads from a spare piece of the material and to use these to make the fringe, either on their own or combined with some of the embroidery threads used on the main item.

1 Work the edging stitch using a firm thread such as cotton perle.

2 Cut a bundle of threads to twice the required length of the tassel, and fold them in half. Pass the loop of threads through a loop of the Armenian edging stitch with the aid of a crochet hook, then put both ends of the bundle through the loop, pulling tight. Repeat along the row, spacing the tassels evenly or unevenly as you wish.

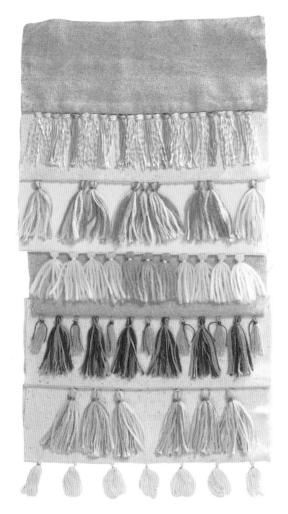

A selection of basic and looped tassels

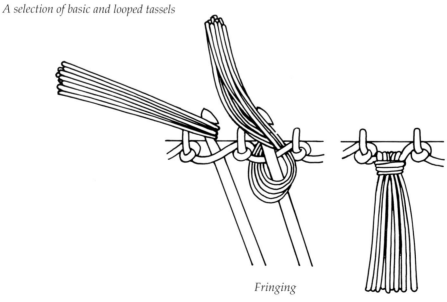

Fringing

BUTTONS

Decorative buttons add a lovely finishing touch to a piece of embroidery, and can be used in combination with a short loop of machine-wrapped cord as a toggle-type fastening. The buttons are made from a length of machine-wrapped cord or a machine-wrapped pipe-cleaner. Use a length of firm string and a piece of fine wire for the cord, as it needs to be fairly stiff. A length of 13-15 cm (5–6 in) will make a medium-sized button.

1 Wrap the string and wire or pipe-cleaner with a close machine zigzag, as described for machine-wrapped cords (see page 116).

2 To form the button, start in the centre and coil the wrapped cord or pipe-cleaner round and round, adding stitches in matching thread as you go to secure the button.

3 Repeat to make as many buttons as you need, and stitch them to the embroidered item in the usual way.

TOGGLES

Ribbon toggles make an attractive fastening on bags or clothes. As with the buttons, they can be used in combination with a loop of machine-wrapped cord.

1 Cut a short length of firm ribbon. Wrap it tightly round a needle, and secure the end with a little glue. Remove the needle.

2 Add further decoration by hand-wrapping either with thread in a matching or contrasting colour, or with thin ribbon caught in place with a few stitches. This added decoration has the advantage of making the toggle more durable and hard-wearing.

3 Make as many toggles as required and attach them to the embroidered item.

A selection of buttons and ribbon toggles

LIST OF SUPPLIERS

Art Van Go
16 Hollybush Lane
Datchworth
Hertfordshire SG3 6RE
(Markal Paint Sticks and
fabric paints)

Campden Needlecraft
Centre
High Street
Chipping Campden
Gloucestershire
(General embroidery
supplies)

De Havilland Embroidery
27 Old Gloucester Street
London WC1 3XX
(Hand-dyed variegated
rayon threads)

John Lewis & Co.
278–306 Oxford Street
London W1A 1EX
(and branches)
(Ribbons and fabrics)

Maple Textiles
188-90 Maple Road
Penge
London SE20 8HT
(Water-soluble fabric)

Pongées Silk
184-6 Old Street
London EC1V 9FR
(Silk fabrics)

Ribbons Design
42 Lake View
Edgware
Hertfordshire HA8 7RU
(Ribbons by mail order)

Shades at Mace & Nairn
89 Crane Street
Salisbury
Wiltshire SP1 2PY
(General embroidery
supplies)

Silken Strands
33 Linksway
Gatley
Cheadle
Cheshire SK8 4LA
(Hand- and machine-
embroidery threads)

Voirrey Embroidery Centre
Brimstage Hall
Wirral L63 6JA
(General embroidery
supplies)

Adelaide Walker
2 Mill Yard Workshops
Otley Mills
Ilkley Road
Otley
West Yorkshire LS21 3JP
(Dyed fleeces)

George Weil & Sons
18 Hanson Street
London W1P 7DB
(Fabric paints, dyes and
equipment)

George Weil & Sons Ltd
The Warehouse
Reading Arch Road
Redhill
Surrey RH1 1HG
(Fabric paints, dyes and
equipment by mail order)

Whaleys (Bradford) Ltd
Harris Court
Great Horton
Bradford
West Yorkshire BD7 4EQ
(Huge range of fabrics)

Wingham Woolwork
70 Main Street
Wentworth
Rotherham
South Yorkshire S62 6TN
(Hand-carders)

FURTHER READING

Butler, Anne *The Batsford Encyclopaedia of Embroidery Stitches* (B.T. Batsford)

Campbell-Harding, Valerie *Fabric Painting for Embroidery* (B.T Batsford)

Harker, Gail *Machine Embroidery* (Merehurst)

Jerstop and Kohlmark, *The Textile Design Book* (Cassell)

Needlework School, *Practical Study Group* (Windward)

Snook, Barbara *Embroidery Stitches* (B.T. Batsford)

Walpole, Lois *Basket Weaving* (HarperCollins)

Watts, Pamela *Machine Embroidery: New Ideas and Techniques* (B. T. Batsford)

Welsh, Nancy *Tassels: The Fanciful Embellishment* (Cassell)

The World of Embroidery, a quarterly magazine published by the Embroiderers' Guild, PO Box 42b, East Molesey, Surrey KT8 9BB.